THE

WF
—
PB

COOKBOOK

THE WF PB COOKBOOK

WITHDRAWN

100 RECIPES TO ENJOY THE WHOLE-FOOD, PLANT-BASED DIET

JUSTIN WEBER

PHOTOGRAPHY BY ANDREW PURCELL

ROCKRIDGE PRESS

Interior and Cover Designer: Monica Cheng
Art Producer: Sara Feinstein
Editor: Rachel Feldman

Photography © 2020 Andrew Purcell. Food styling by Carrie Purcell.
Illustrations used under license from iStock.com.
Cover: Chickpea Coconut Curry (page 104)

ISBN: Print 978-1-64739-618-3 | eBook 978-1-64739-386-1

R0

This book is dedicated to my aunt Brenda.
Her joyful spirit in the kitchen inspired me to cook,
and her memory lives on in my kitchen today.

*

contents

introduction

In my early 30s, I weighed close to 400 pounds. Doctors warned me I wouldn't live to see my 40s because of high blood pressure and cholesterol. I was on the path to developing type 2 diabetes.

When my son was born, I realized I had to make a change—not only so I could be an active dad, but also simply to be alive to watch him grow up. Changing my relationship with food has been the most important part of my health journey. For years, I mistreated my body with high-sugar, high-fat, highly processed foods, and it nearly killed me. My transition to the whole-food, plant-based diet, however, came as a result of my weight loss. As I lost weight and reflected on my food choices, I realized how much better I felt when eating real food I made at home. I cooked more, learned about food and nutrition, and started to create my own recipes based on what I was learning.

My goal is to provide a creative and holistic approach to cooking that empowers others to establish a healthy, sustainable lifestyle. I want others to experience the same joy I have creating and eating a diverse range of food that is visually appealing, tasty, and nutritious. Eating a whole-food, plant-based diet is not a sacrifice—it's life-giving, and eating this way has helped me honor and respect both food and myself. Food is vital to our human heritage and my goal is to give people the needed tools to get into the kitchen and create.

There are more than 20,000 edible plants on this planet, but we typically eat only about 20 of them. The whole-food, plant-based diet is a showcase of variety, and the more you learn about fruits, vegetables, and flavor combinations, the more you'll want to experience. So you won't be eating less or sacrificing flavor—instead, you'll be adding even more colorful ingredients to your plate, each with its own unique flavor profile. This is not a health book or a meal plan, and you don't need to eat whole-food, plant-based for every meal, but making these recipes and learning about plant-based nutrition will help you understand how eating more plants leads to better health.

The recipes in this book are just a taste of what the whole-food, plant-based diet has to offer. The 100 recipes here cover everything from breakfast sweets and savories, richly flavored entrées, and even staple foods such as gravy and pickles. As you make these recipes, you'll learn a variety of cooking techniques to enhance the overall flavor and nutrition of your meals, like oil-free sautéing and tempering spices for more flavor. The recipes I selected for this book cover many flavors, ranging from classic American comfort foods like mac and cheese to Indian-inspired cuisine like masoor dal.

The purpose of the wide range of recipes is to help you experience a variety of plants and spices and how, together, they can create so many different flavors, textures, and aromas. It is truly my hope that you, too, will fall in love with the whole-food, plant-based diet, and that you'll learn not only to be comfortable cooking with plants but also confident.

CREAMY MUSHROOM PIZZA ★ PAGE 134

back to the roots with WFPB

Welcome to the whole-food, plant-based diet! This diet is about filling your plate to the brim with delicious foods that are colorful, fresh, and easy to fit into any lifestyle. Part 1 introduces you to the principles of this way of eating, the health benefits of using whole foods for your meals, new ingredients and ways of cooking with them, a variety of tips and tricks for plant-based shopping, and even chopping techniques. This is an exciting culinary adventure you're about to embark on, and what you'll learn here will prepare you for success in your new whole-food, plant-based kitchen.

SWEET POTATO
GNOCCHI ★ PAGE 118

– 1 –

FOOD IN ITS NATURAL STATE

The whole-food, plant-based diet goes back to the roots of home cooking by using ingredients in their natural state. In this chapter, you'll learn everything you need to know about this way of eating. You'll see that the whole-food, plant-based diet is more than a diet—it's a lifestyle—and by enjoying food that is close to nature, you are giving your body the fuel it needs for sustainable health.

What's Up with WFPB?

Over the past two decades there has been an exponential rise in trendy diets, weight loss companies, and low-calorie food products. However, two-thirds of adults in America remain obese. Shockingly, the more we invest in the health industry, the sharper the decline we see in overall health. Everyone wants longevity and health, but so much information makes it confusing to know what to do or what to believe. The best way to understand health is to study those who are healthy.

In 2004, *The China Study* was published based on data collected over a span of 20 years by Cornell University, Oxford University, and the Chinese Academy of Preventive Medicine. More than 6,500 adults in China were given questionnaires on their habits and patterns of living, blood tests, and regular medical checkups. The researchers found that those who followed a whole-food, plant-based diet had little to no cardiovascular problems, rare instances of cancer, and the majority were free from diabetes, obesity, and diseases affecting autoimmunity, bone, kidney, eye, and brain health. The data showed that the majority of life-threatening health complications were linked to consuming refined sugars, added sodium, unhealthy fats, and animal products. The study's conclusion was simply that people who ate the most plant-based foods were the healthiest.

You might ask yourself why you haven't heard of this study or others like it. Companies who market quick-fix products and plans rely on people buying their products and not making sustainable changes. We are bombarded with advertisements that feature flashy labels, gimmicky names, guarantees of weight loss, and promises of fast and easy health, but we aren't given the information to take power into our own hands. As consumers have better access to nutrition facts, companies develop strategies to redirect attention and design new ways of interpreting nutrition. We are sold fat-free, low-sodium, high-protein products and we begin to believe that health is based on these qualifiers.

The whole-food, plant-based diet is gaining popularity because more people seek long-term health benefits that are holistic, easy to understand and apply, and based on food that isn't artificial or processed. Food in its natural state is full of colors and flavors that are not meant to trick our brains or bodies! Your body will respond to this almost immediately. You will feel pleasantly full for longer and have sustained energy throughout the day. The long-term health benefits, even more impressive, include stopping heart disease, reversing type 2 diabetes, and reducing the risk of certain types of cancer. The whole-food, plant-based diet gives you the power to change your life.

* bonus benefits *

There are many benefits to the whole-food, plant-based diet beyond reversing life-threatening health complications.

1. **More food for people.** More than 40 percent of land in the United States is used to feed livestock! By choosing plant-based foods, you use less land to produce more food. This means we could grow more fruits, vegetables, and grains for humans to eat.

2. **Positive environmental impact.** You can feel good knowing you will help minimize agricultural usage, save fresh water, and reduce toxins produced from industrial processing facilities.

3. **Better mood.** Plant-based diets are high in brain-friendly vitamins, such as folate and B_6, which boost your mood. No wonder people feel happier eating this way!

4. **Healthy blood.** Your body produces all the cholesterol it needs, and eating animal products adds cholesterol that clogs arteries and raises blood pressure. The best way to lower cholesterol is to stop eating it.

5. **Better digestion.** Peristalsis is the constriction and relaxation of your intestines, which is how food moves through your lower digestive tract. This necessary action occurs when you eat fiber-rich foods, such as grains, fruit, and vegetables.

6. **Better complexion.** Meat and animal products like milk are high in a certain amino acids that trigger your body to produce excess sebum, or oil, which leads to acne breakouts. Eating a variety of plant-based whole foods gives your body the vitamins and minerals it needs for healthy, glowing skin.

7. **Lasting energy.** Plants are high in vitamins and minerals, phytonutrients, antioxidants, and fiber. They are easy to digest, release energy gradually, and you'll feel the effects longer than from foods loaded with refined sugar and fats.

The Whole-Food, Plant-Based Diet

When we hear the word "diet," we immediately think about meal plans, sad-looking dinner plates, and giving up foods we enjoy. The whole-food, plant-based diet is not a weight loss program intended to take away the enjoyment we get from food. Instead, it's a way of eating that focuses on natural, plant-based foods that are not heavily processed to give your body plenty of vitamins and minerals. It's a way to bring life to your meals through colors, flavors, and variety. This way of eating is centered on understanding and harnessing the nutritional benefits from plants, including vegetables, tubers, fruits, seeds and nuts, whole grains, and legumes such as chickpeas and lentils.

100% Plants

The foundation of this diet is using plants and plant-based ingredients as the primary or sole source of nutrition. Plants provide the vitamins, minerals, phytonutrients, protein, and fiber you need to maintain health and fight off illness. These natural ingredients give you everything your body needs while being both visually pleasing and delicious.

Whole Foods

Whole foods are foods eaten in their natural state, or as close to it as possible, and that haven't been treated with chemicals, refined, or enhanced through industrial means. These foods are easier for your body to digest and benefit from, while being lower in calories, higher in fiber, and more conducive to maintaining a healthy body weight. Some examples of whole foods are fruits, vegetables, nuts, seeds, legumes (beans, peas, lentils), and whole grains (brown rice, quinoa, oats). Eating whole foods has been shown to lower the risk of heart disease and diabetes, and, in some cases, reverse these complications.

SOS

Salt, oil, and sugar are all linked to health complications and are the three main additives common in processed foods. The sections on page 8 break down the risks.

PLANT-BASED SWAPS

Eggs	▶	• 1 tablespoon ground flaxseed mixed with 3 tablespoons water • ¼ cup silken tofu • ¼ cup unsweetened applesauce
Fats/oils	▶	• Avocado • Ground flaxseed • Nut butters
Milk	▶	• Blended, soaked raw cashews • Nut-based and coconut milks • Unsweetened oat milk
Protein from meat	▶	• Beans • Legumes and pulses • Nut butters
Salt	▶	• Garlic • Celery and green bell pepper • Herbs and spice such as cumin, oregano, and paprika
Sugar	▶	• Dried dates • Ripe bananas • Tomato paste

SALT

Salt, also referred to as sodium, is added to processed foods to lengthen shelf stability and add flavor. Consuming excess sodium increases blood pressure, which increases your risk for heart failure, stroke, stomach cancer, and kidney disease. Around 30 percent of Americans will develop high blood pressure in their lifetime, and minimizing sodium is a way to decrease your risk for health complications.

OIL

The consumption of oil has increased dramatically in the last 50 years as more food products have been created. Even though less-refined oils like olive oil contain heart-healthy omega-6 and omega-3 fatty acids, the overconsumption of oils promotes heart disease. Additionally, most oils, like corn, canola, and soy, are created using a high-heat process, which oxidizes the oils and creates free radicals that can lead to cancer. Most food products today have highly processed oils added to them, or these oils are used for cooking.

SUGAR

Sugar shows up in the most unexpected packaged food products, like peanut butter, soup, marinara, and even bread. In the United States, added sugars account for nearly 20 percent of daily calories for adults, putting people at risk for type 2 diabetes, heart disease, acne, and certain cancers. Making your own food from natural ingredients is a simple way of eliminating the dangers accompanied with consuming added sugar.

Need-to-Know Nutrition

Learning about all the vitamins, minerals, phytonutrients, and antioxidants from a diverse source of plants is one of the most exciting parts of transitioning to the whole-food, plant-based diet. We all know the adage: An apple a day keeps the doctor away. But we typically don't look beyond the singsong sentence. A fresh apple includes fiber for gut health and digestion; the phytonutrient quercetin, which has been linked to reducing the effects of asthma, certain cancers, and coronary heart disease; and polyphenol antioxidants, which can lower the risk of type 2 diabetes. Understanding the nutrition and positive effects of the whole-food, plant-based diet is powerful, and that knowledge will help you plan your meals to get the most from your food.

Protein, Carbs, and Fats

As you transition to the whole-food, plant-based diet, you might have questions concerning the macronutrients needed for a healthy body. Having even a general understanding of the three macronutrients is important for everyone.

PROTEIN

Protein is essential for cell production and aids in feeling full longer. The recommended minimum protein intake is a modest 0.36 grams per pound of body weight, or, on average, 15 to 25 percent of daily calories from a protein source. This number fluctuates based on activity level, age, and sex. The recipes in this book offer a wide range of protein sources that can easily be swapped from one recipe to another, and the inclusion of complete proteins, containing all essential amino acids, are a focus in the entrée section, chapter 6.

CARBS

Carbs are the macronutrient most diets eliminate because they are commonly associated with weight gain. However, the recommended amount of carbohydrates for an adult is between 45 to 65 percent of daily calories (the amount in grams depends on individual caloric intake and will vary widely based on age, activity level, weight, and sex). The problem with carbs isn't in their nature; it's in their production. Refined grains, like those in white breads, have fiber and protein stripped, which causes them to be digested too quickly and leads to a rapid rise and fall of blood sugar. Whole food is unrefined and, therefore, contains the fiber necessary to promote even blood sugar levels and less frequent cravings for snacks.

FAT

Fat is misunderstood—good fats are a necessary macronutrient for brain health, nutrient absorption, and positive hormone production. Between 20 and 35 percent of your daily calories should be from fat for brain health and proper vitamin and mineral absorption (the amount in grams depends on individual caloric intake and will vary widely based on age, activity level, weight, and sex). However, it is easy to overdo the fat if you are cooking and baking with a lot of oil. Part of the whole-food, plant-based diet is reducing or eliminating refined oils and replacing them with plant-based ingredients. Essential dietary fat can be found in avocados, chia seeds, flaxseed, and nuts.

Vitamins and Supplements

The recipes throughout this book are stand-alone and are not a meal plan. As you plan your meals, consider diverse sources of macronutrients and micronutrients. By eating whole-food, plant-based meals, you will get a range of vitamins and minerals from a variety of vegetables and fruits. Yes, you can even get iron from dark leafy greens and vitamin B_{12} from plant-based sources like nutritional yeast and tempeh. However, it is beneficial to consider taking supplements or using fortified ingredients that contain B_{12}, iron, and vitamins D and K_2, as well as omega-3 fatty acids. Although it is possible to get all the recommended vitamins and minerals from foods, these just mentioned are often lacking for everyone, regardless of diet, according to medical research.

Getting to Know the Ingredients

Venturing into the whole-food, plant-based diet is exciting because it gives you opportunities to enjoy and discover brand-new foods! This section is all about understanding just a small portion of the vast variety of ingredients available to you within the whole-food, plant-based diet.

Green-coded ingredients are those you'll be consuming most often, whereas the **yellow-coded** ones you'll enjoy occasionally.

Root Vegetables

Root vegetables grow under the earth, which makes them rich in a variety of vitamins and minerals. Each provides its own unique nutritional benefits and offers a range of sweet to earthy to spicy flavors. They are also the easiest fresh ingredients to store, because they prefer cool, dark, open places and have a long shelf life after harvest. Root vegetables are also the most affordable ingredients to stock in your pantry.

- Beet
- Carrot
- Garlic
- Potato
- Radish
- Sweet Potato
- Turnip

Vegetables

We often put anything that's not a root vegetable and not clearly a fruit in the "vegetable" category. However, we all have that one friend who corrects you when you call a pumpkin a vegetable, because, technically, it is a fruit. For the sake of tradition and clarity, we will include cruciferous, marrow, and edible plant stems as vegetables. The broad spectrum of nutritional benefits, flavors, and textures in this category is explored more in the recipes. Vegetables as a whole are high in vitamins and minerals and should make up the majority of what you consume throughout your day. The vegetables in these categories are best enjoyed fresh and most should be kept refrigerated.

[Vegetables continued]

Cruciferous Vegetables

- Broccoli
- Brussels sprouts
- Cabbage
- Cauliflower

Marrow Vegetables

- Cucumber
- Pumpkin
- Squash
- Zucchini

Edible Plant Stems

- Asparagus
- Celery
- Leek

Greens

Leafy greens are often an afterthought, or garnish, when making a meal or plating a dish. These vegetables are just as necessary as the rest listed here for well-rounded nutrition. They are also often affordable and they add texture and visual interest to a meal. The darker the green, the higher in calcium it is, and many of these leafy greens provide high amounts of fiber.

- Arugula
- Beet greens
- Bok choy
- Kale
- Microgreens[1]
- Romaine lettuce
- Spinach
- Swiss chard

[1] **Microgreens** contain up to 40 times more nutrients than their leafy green counterparts and are high in vitamins C, E, and K. Arugula, bok choy, romaine lettuce, and Swiss chard grow from small seeds, which you can grow right in your home kitchen.

Fruit

Fruit is important both as an ingredient and a ready-to-eat snack. The bright, diverse colors of fresh fruit, along with their natural sweetness, make any meal more visually appealing and appetizing. Fruits offer many health benefits and the vitamins, minerals, and antioxidants vary based on type of fruit and even color.

- Apple
- Avocado
- Banana
- Blueberries
- Cranberry
- Grapefruit
- Jackfruit[2]
- Mango
- Pomegranate
- Strawberry

[2] **Jackfruit**, native fruit to South India, is similar in taste to a mild pineapple and unusually large when grown to maturity. Jackfruit has gained popularity over the past few years because, when purchased as "young green jackfruit in brine," it can be used in savory dishes to mimic the texture of pulled pork or chicken.

Beans and Legumes

Beans and legumes are a staple in the whole-food, plant-based diet and will be used in many recipes throughout this book. They are high in fiber and protein and provide necessary B vitamins and lasting energy throughout your day. The benefit of this category is you can purchase these ingredients dried for a lower cost and cook them as needed to prep for meals during the week.

- Black beans
- Chickpeas[3]
- Great northern beans
- Kidney beans
- Lentils
- Peanuts
- Peas
- Pinto beans

[3] **Chickpeas** are rich in fiber and protein, containing 15 grams of protein per cooked cup, and are beneficial in reducing blood sugar levels compared to other high-carb foods.

Whole Grains

Grains are also a pantry staple and are used in many recipes in this book. The whole-food, plant-based diet focuses on keeping grains intact rather than stripping them of their bran and germ. White breads are made using a flour that is primarily the endosperm, the starchy carb. Without the other two parts of the grain, your body processes it too quickly, which leads to a spike in blood sugar. The grains listed here are often found milled into flour, but you can cook and enjoy them as a whole grain.

- Barley
- Brown rice
- Buckwheat
- Bulgur wheat
- Corn (dried)
- Farro
- Oats
- Quinoa
- Sorghum
- Whole-grain rye
- Whole wheat

Herbs and Spices

The best thing a home cook can do is to learn about herbs and spices and how to use them to enhance foods' natural flavors. The difference between a good meal and a great one is how you've utilized spices to create complexity and balance. Also, using a variety of flavorful herbs and spices helps reduce, even eliminate, salt from your cooking. Fresh herbs are best stored in your refrigerator's crisper drawer in a plastic bag and should be used within a week of purchase. Spices are most pungent when used within 3 to 6 months of purchase. If you have that jar of basil from 10 years ago still hanging around, you might want to get a fresh one.

- Basil
- Cilantro
- Cinnamon
- Coriander, ground
- Ginger, ground
- Nutmeg, ground
- Nutritional yeast[4]
- Oregano

- Paprika: Hungarian,[5] Spanish, and smoked
- Parsley
- Peppercorns
- Red pepper flakes
- Rosemary
- Sage
- Scallions or spring onions
- Thyme
- Vanilla, extract and whole beans

[4] **Nutritional yeast** is deactivated yeast with a cheesy, nutty taste. It's high in protein and B vitamins. It is great for soups, salads, and plant-based cheeses.

[5] **Hungarian paprika** is the fourth most consumed spice in the world and it's the national spice of Hungary. In America, when paprika is labeled "Hungarian," it refers to one of the eight grades of the spice *édesnemes*, which is noted for its slight sweetness, pungent flavor, and bright red color. It is used often in my recipes for those qualities.

Nuts and Other Seeds

Using nuts and seeds in a recipe is an easy way to boost protein while eating a plant-based diet; however, at 100 calories per tablespoon of nut butter, it is easy to overconsume when making a snack or a sandwich. The best way to purchase nuts and seeds is in bulk, and raw if possible, so you control the roasting, which adds to their flavor.

- Almonds
- Cashews
- Chia seeds[6]
- Flaxseed[7]
- Hemp seeds
- Peanuts
- Pecans
- Pistachios
- Pumpkin seeds
- Sesame seeds
- Sunflower seeds
- Walnuts

[6] **Chia seeds**—with only 1 ounce (about 2 tablespoons) of chia seeds, you can check off your daily recommended amount of omega-3 fatty acids. You can also use chia seeds as an egg replacer when baking: Mix 1 tablespoon of chia seeds and 3 tablespoons of water per egg.

[7] **Flaxseed** is a common ingredient in plant-based baking. When combined with water, it gels to create a binding product similar to egg. The soaked flaxseed also ensures your baked goods keep the proper amount of hydration rather than drying out.

Minimally Processed Whole Soy Products

When eaten in moderation, soy products offer a complete protein, fiber, and heart-healthy fats. Even though they are processed, these products have minimal additional ingredients. The main debate regarding soy products is whether soy promotes or decreases estrogen levels in the human body; however, based on many studies, soy has been shown safe to consume several times a week, especially when replacing red and processed meats.

- Edamame
- Miso[8]
- Soy milk
- Tamari[9]
- Tempeh
- Tofu

[8] **Miso**, a common ingredient in Asian cooking, has made its way into plant-based recipes to add umami and cheeselike flavor. There are two main types of miso: red and yellow (or mellow). Both are made from fermented soybeans, but red miso has a stronger flavor and saltiness due to its longer fermentation time.

[9] **Tamari**, like soy sauce, is made from fermented soybeans. The main difference is that tamari does not contain wheat, which makes it a good gluten-free option. Tamari is generally darker in color, richer in flavor, and less salty than its soy sauce counterpart.

Natural Sweeteners

When transitioning to the whole-food, plant-based diet, the first major change to be made is reducing or eliminating refined sugars from cooking and baking. We have been trained, in America, to overconsume refined sugars, like high-fructose corn syrup. Your body processes refined sugar too quickly, which causes blood sugar spikes that change insulin production and use. There are, however, natural sweeteners that can satisfy your sweet tooth. Many of these sweeteners offer other nutritional benefits, like essential vitamins and minerals.

- Carrots
- Coconut sugar
- Cooked beets
- Dried dates

- ° Maple syrup
- ° Molasses
- ° Yacon syrup[10]

[10] **Yacon syrup**, made from the South American yacon plant, contains 40 to 50 percent fructool- igosaccharide, a sugar molecule the human body does not digest like refined sugar. It is naturally sweet, dark in color, and has a similar consistency to molasses.

Healthy ≠ Bland

Food is truly powerful. The intoxicating aromas from spices and fresh ingredi- ents in a homemade shakshuka, apple pie, or masala chai can turn a house into a home. Truly, good food is a necessary part of the human experience and it requires little skill and experience for the home cook to create meals and memories from simple, real ingredients.

The whole-food, plant-based diet elevates natural ingredients to create fresh, vibrant meals that also just happen to be full of nutrients. The dishes in this book not only bring out the natural flavors of whole foods, they are built around the five main flavor components: salty, sweet, bitter, sour, and umami.

Here are a few important ways this diet will help you enjoy food even more.

You'll learn more about ingredients. Cooking this way introduces you to new ingredients, which allows you to become more confident and creative in the kitchen. Working with new ingredients can mean learning about other cuisines and cultures. All this helps make eating much more than the simple consump- tion of calories.

You'll learn to build better meals. Cooking with real, whole ingredients teaches you new cooking techniques and flavor nuances. You'll learn how to chop and cook items so they achieve the best texture as well as how to combine spices and herbs with different foods to enjoy new flavor profiles.

You'll recalibrate how you taste and enjoy food. Fast foods and packaged foods overload our senses with artificial sweeteners and high sodium contents. Transitioning to enjoying natural ingredients gives the brain the opportunity to experience food at a level that is not a trick or disguise. Your palate expands and you're able to discern a variety of flavors beyond simply sweet and salty.

-2-

YOUR WFPB KITCHEN

Now that you've learned all about the food, what about the logistics? This chapter will show you how to use what you learned in Chapter 1 to start cooking! You'll learn how to use ripe produce to maximize flavor, how to keep costs down at the grocery store, and how to sauté without oil. The tips, tools, and techniques in this chapter will help you start incorporating WFPB into your lifestyle right away.

Smart Shopping

The basis for eating a whole-food, plant-based diet is to make sure you're getting everything your body needs from minimally or unprocessed sources. It's vital to plan your shopping list in advance to ensure you purchase foods to meet your nutritional needs and avoid unnecessary purchases that will lead to food waste. It's also helpful to learn where to find quality ingredients, and even more beneficial to use multiple shopping sources, if you can.

Sourcing quality ingredients

This is a comparative term. A quality ingredient means one at the peak of freshness from a reputable seller and that will provide the most benefit. We can use this to describe any ingredient in the whole-food, plant-based diet.

- **Shop at your local farmers' market.** Not only will you find ingredients that are fresh and seasonal, but they also come from members of your own community.

- **Buy organic and GMO-free.** Untampered ingredients are the premise of the whole-food, plant-based diet. If a product is genetically modified or loaded with toxic chemicals, it takes away from the overall integrity of the product and your goal for eating WFPB.

- **Shop for the seasons.** When you work with in-season ingredients, you're using them at their highest quality. To preserve out-of-season ingredients, extra steps are required between your food and your plate, and companies often resort to artificial means of ripening.

Keeping costs down

A whole-food, plant-based diet doesn't have to be expensive. When you plan your shopping trips, you get the most for your money by purchasing only what you need.

- **Buy in bulk.** Lots of dry ingredients can be found in the bulk section of your grocery store. Grains, nuts, beans, etc. can all be purchased as bulk items. Shopping this way also cuts down on packaging and gives you more for your money.

- **Shop the sales.** The more you shop for the whole-food, plant-based diet, the more you'll find yourself browsing the sale ads for your local grocers. When pantry items are on sale, stock up! When there's a buy-one, get-one sale, stock up or swap items to add variety to your cart.

- **Avoid impulse purchases.** Shop along the perimeter of your grocery store for bulk foods, produce, and other fresh items first. Impulse purchase items are generally found in the center of the store and can be avoided to save money.

Minimizing leftovers

It is easy to get excited about all the cooking you're doing now that you've unlocked the joy of the whole-food, plant-based diet, but too much cooking leads to food waste and an overfull refrigerator.

- **Make a visible plan.** When you plan your week of meals, hang your meal list in a visible place for you and others to enjoy. A large calendar, dry-erase board, or chalkboard is a great way to make your eating plan accessible to all.

- **Have a leftover day.** If you do the bulk of your meal prep and cooking on Sunday, aim for a midweek day to use up the leftovers in your refrigerator. It's fun to create a meal from the bits and pieces of your week's creations. When all else fails, dump things into a bowl and call it a salad.

- **Keep it simple.** Not every meal needs to be time-intensive, complex, or driven by a recipe. A simple grain bowl or soup uses up odds and ends and minimizes the need to make space for storage. Make it a goal to have a meal during the week that won't make leftovers.

✳ ripe with opportunity ✳

Fruits and vegetables at their peak ripeness offer us their best flavor, are easier to digest, and their antioxidants are able to be absorbed properly. As you transition to the whole-food, plant-based diet, you will become a modern-day gatherer in your grocery store—and feel comfortable and confident sniffing berries, thumping melons, and bending asparagus. The general rule for all fresh fruits and vegetables is they are best when vibrantly colored.

▶ **Asparagus.** The size of the stem is not the determining factor when selecting fresh asparagus. Look for firm, bright green stems and a hue of violet. If you can snap them, they are freshest.

▶ **Avocado.** Avocado is one of the few fruits not to ripen while still on the tree. Typically, you'll purchase avocado while underripe and hard, then allow it to ripen on your counter. A ripe avocado will have a slight give when squeezed and the color under the stem will be green.

▶ **Banana.** Bananas are ripe when covered in black spots and smell sweet.

▶ **Broccoli.** The best way to check broccoli is to pick it up. If it feels heavy for its size, it is fresh. A head should have tightly packed florets and be evenly green in appearance.

▶ **Brussels sprouts.** Smaller Brussels sprouts will be more tender and sweeter than large ones. Avoid Brussels sprouts with yellowing leaves or spots, or those that are dull in color.

- **Dragon fruit or pitaya.** Choose a dragon fruit that is vibrant and even in color. When squeezed, it should be firm to allow a day or two to ripen at home.

- **Green beans.** A green bean should be green and free of blemishes. Test a bean at the store by trying to snap it in half. If it bends, it is over-ripe; if it has an audible snap, it is ripe.

- **Mango.** Test the ripeness of a mango by gently squeezing it. If it gives slightly, the flesh inside is ripe.

- **Melon.** A juicy melon will feel heavy, have a sweet smell, dull rind appearance, and will sound hollow when tapped. The best watermelons have some sting marks from bees.

- **Pineapple.** Ripe pineapples have a distinctive pineapple scent at the bottom of the fruit when sniffed. The leaves will be brighter green, the shell will be firm rather than hard, and the fruit will have a slight give when squeezed.

Storage 101

Understanding how to properly store your ingredients and fresh produce will make a big difference in how you shop, help cut down on food waste (saving money), and maximize nutritional benefits. Not having to throw food away because of spoilage is an easy way to keep your shopping costs in check. You can organize your pantry, freezer, refrigerator, and counter space using a few tips, tricks, and tools.

Pantry

- Expiration dates are a guideline that should be followed. When purchasing pantry items, check the expiration date or the "packed on" date. Milled flour is typically good for up to 1 year stored in an airtight container.

- Glass canning jars are an inexpensive way to store pantry items like nuts, seeds, dried fruits, and specialty flours. Purchase them in a variety of sizes. Amber-colored jars protect contents like spices from light, because light can deteriorate ingredients faster.

- Organize your shelves to avoid cross-contamination, damage to packaging, and crushing ingredients. Store taller items in the back or use shelving inserts so you can see everything you have.

- Avoid using counters for storage because the more cluttered your kitchen becomes, the less likely you'll want to use it. A clean, chaos-free kitchen invites you in and promotes creativity.

- Bread will become stale quickly in the refrigerator and should be stored on the countertop or in the pantry. However, you can also freeze bread for long-term storage.

- Dried spices should be kept out of the refrigerator due to its moist environment and the variety of odors they can pick up there. Store in a place without sunlight, like a cupboard or the pantry, for best results.

Freezer

- Do not overstock your freezer. The last thing you want is to forget about your food or let it get crushed. Plus, overstocking a freezer can cause it to run less efficiently, meaning the correct storage temperature may not be kept consistent.

- Remove as much air as possible before sealing freezer bags. If you plan to store a lot in your freezer, a vacuum sealer is a good investment. The other two ways to remove air from a bag are to suck it out with your mouth or dip the bag into a bowl of water and seal once all air has been expelled.

- Organize your freezer into compartments or sections. This will help you quickly find common items like fruits, baked goods, meals, and vegetables.

- Clearly mark what's in your bags and containers: Add a piece of masking tape to the container and use a marker to record what's in it!

Refrigerator

- Line crisper drawers with paper towels to absorb extra moisture, keeping produce crisper and fresh longer. Replace the paper towel when you restock your crisper with high-moisture produce like herbs, leafy greens, and peppers.

- Remove produce from grocery bags before refrigerating to avoid moisture buildup. Keep produce in open mesh organizing baskets or loose in the crisper drawer.

- If your produce comes in a sealed bag at the grocery store, it should be kept moist and stored in a sealed bag at home.

- Use refrigerator door shelves for condiments and other more stable items that don't mold or spoil as quickly. The door is the warmest part of your refrigerator.

- The back of the shelves is the coldest part of your refrigerator and vegetables can freeze if stored along that back wall.

quick guide to storing fresh produce

*   *

Fresh fruits and vegetables have a short window of peak ripeness and it's important to ensure your food investment is ready to eat when you're ready to eat it. Unless otherwise noted, don't wash your produce before storing it; washing adds moisture and removes the protective layer of soil. Some produce will spoil faster in the refrigerator and should be stored either on the counter or in a cool, dark place like your pantry or basement.

▸ **Avocados.** Refrigerate avocados once they are ripe and ready to be eaten. Chilling them prolongs the ripening process, which can occur too quickly at room temperature, causing them to spoil.

▸ **Bananas.** Keep bananas on the counter and away from other fruits and vegetables. Bananas emit ethylene gas in high amounts, which causes other produce to ripen too quickly. However, you can use this to your advantage by placing a banana in a bag with your underripe stone fruits. To freeze them, peel and cut bananas, then place in a single layer on a parchment-paper lined baking sheet to freeze. Once frozen, transfer to an airtight bag for longer storage. This method prevents your bananas from freezing into a solid block. They can be used for banana breads, smoothies, or nice cream.

▸ **Berries.** Keep fresh berries, unwashed, in your refrigerator. Washing berries adds extra moisture, which speeds decay, so it's best to wash them only before eating. If you freeze berries, wash and dry them well before storing. It is best to freeze berries in an airtight bag, frozen in a single layer, and stacked in your freezer.

- ▶ **Cauliflower.** Wash, dry, and cut florets. Freeze them in an airtight bag and remove as much air as possible. Frozen, then thawed, cauliflower will be softer than fresh, but will work well for baking, soups, and even smoothies.

- ▶ **Fresh herbs.** Leafy herbs love moisture, because they are, essentially, still a living plant until they run out of water. Trim the ends and place the stems in a jar with a little water and refrigerate.

- ▶ **Garlic.** Stored in a cool, well-ventilated place, but not the refrigerator.

- ▶ **Green beans.** Wash then blanch your green beans by boiling them in water for 1 minute. Immediately transfer to cold water to stop the cooking. Dry using a towel and freeze in a sealable plastic bag.

- ▶ **Leafy greens.** Wash the leaves well and pat dry before refrigerating. Refrigerate in a plastic bag with a few paper towels if storing for more than 1 or 2 days. Freezing washed and dried leafy greens changes their texture, breaking down the cellular structure. This works to your advantage, because your frozen greens will be softer for soups, stews, and purees.

- ▶ **Melons.** Keep fresh melons on the counter.

- ▶ **Mushrooms.** Store them in the refrigerator, preferably in a paper bag to absorb moisture, and only wash before use.

- ▶ **Onions.** Store at room temperature. Refrigerate only after they have been cut.

- ▶ **Potatoes.** Potatoes should be removed from their plastic packaging and stored in a cool, dark, dry part of your house. If they start to sprout, simply pinch off the sprouts. Refrigeration breaks down their starches and dries out the potatoes.

- ▶ **Tomatoes.** Tomatoes should be stored on the counter because the refrigerator's cold air makes them mealy and dulls their flavor.

Essential Tools

After stocking your pantry, equipping your kitchen with essential tools is the next step in getting ready for the cooking adventure you're about to begin. The endless gadgets and gear available in kitchen stores may seem daunting, but once you start to work through the recipes in this book you'll find you can make a lot with a few key tools. Having a professional stand mixer is fun, but pricey gadgets aren't necessary. Here are my recommendations:

Blender, preferably high speed. Many recipes in this book use a blender or food processor for prep work. It may be tempting to purchase a cheaper model, but spending a little extra makes the difference in how long it lasts and the quality of purees it produces. Blenders that boast at least 1,000 watts are recommended because they power through heavy sauces and other recipes with ease.

Immersion blender. This kitchen gadget generally costs between $30 and $40 and lets you puree a pot of hot soup or a sauce without having to transfer batches to an upright blender. They won't get a sauce as creamy as a high-speed blender, but they will save time and stress when working with a large pot of hot tomato sauce.

Pressure cooker. Beans are one of the more time-consuming ingredients on the whole-food, plant-based diet because they require both a long soaking period and boiling time when using the dried variety. A pressure cooker cuts bean prep and cook time to minutes and makes other recipes fast and easy, too. Years ago, pressure cookers were challenging to use and required calibration; in today's kitchen you can enjoy safe and reliable pressure cooking using an electric pressure cooker. When purchasing a pressure cooker, buy a larger-capacity model to allow the option of cooking larger meals.

Sharp knife. One of the first kitchen tools people purchase is a knife block, but the knives in these blocks generally aren't made with high-quality steel and aren't properly balanced. It is a good investment to spend between $75 and $100 on a high-quality chef's knife, made from better steel and with a forging process that produces a blade that stays sharp longer, and a honing rod. Damascus, Japanese, and German blades will last decades with proper care and handling, and will speed prep time, reduce kitchen accidents, and stop hand fatigue. Also, a high-quality steel knife only needs honing between uses and sharpening rarely. If you purchase your knife at a kitchen supply store, they often offer free sharpening for life.

✳ proper knife care ✳

Take care of your knives and they will last a long time and serve you well on your culinary journey—a sharp knife is a safer, more efficient tool. Keeping your knives honed and sharpened helps prevent the blade from slipping while cutting with it, which can lead to kitchen accidents.

Sharpening a kitchen knife is needed infrequently, and only when there is a nick or dent in the blade's edge. Sharpening removes metal from the knife and can create an uneven blade surface if done improperly. There are a few simple methods to keep a knife as sharp as possible:

▸ Hand-wash kitchen knives rather than putting them through the dishwasher. The abrasive dishwashing detergent and contact with other metal objects quickly dulls a blade's edge.

▸ Store the knife on a mounted magnetic strip or in a knife block to avoid contact with other metal objects, such as in a "knife drawer."

▸ Use a honing rod, often included with a knife block package, to straighten and center the blade edge. Hone your knife prior to use for best results. Hold the honing rod upright and on a cutting board (never over food). Slide the knife down the rod starting with the base of the blade and working toward the tip with each downstroke. Hone the knife four to five times on both sides.

Plant-Powered Kitchen Techniques

Throughout this book there are certain techniques you will become familiar with. It is challenging to explain a technique in written directions, but just knowing there is an actual difference between terms takes your cooking from good to great.

Chopping Techniques

Chiffonade. Cutting leafy vegetables into thin strips to be used as a garnish. Stack your leafy greens, like basil, roll tightly like a cigar, and thinly cut perpendicular to the roll. You can use this technique for fresh herbs or leafy vegetables, like romaine and beet greens.

Grating. You can grate harder vegetables using a knife, scraping it down the side of the vegetable to create small flecks and flakes. This technique does not replace a box grater and is helpful when you need a light garnish of carrot and don't want to dirty another cooking utensil.

Mincing, dicing, and chopping. These are the most common cutting terms you'll see throughout the book and all three have different uses, textures, and appearances.

- *Mincing* is the finest cut and used for adding flavor to a dish rather than texture.

- *Dicing* is cutting the vegetable into even pea-size pieces and is used when sautéing or adding a raw crunch.

- *Chopping* is not concerned with evenness and is best used for sauces and soups that will be pureed.

Sheet peeling. Using a vegetable peeler, or a steady hand and sharp knife, cut thin strips of vegetables to use similarly to lasagna noodles. The thin strips cook quickly and hold in ingredients for fresh wraps, taco shells, or noodles.

Spiralizing. Spiralizing isn't the most common cutting method, but it is a way to mimic the texture and appearance of wheat noodles. The easiest means of spiralizing vegetables like zucchini or carrot is to use a spiralizer tool, but you can spiralize vegetables using a Y-shaped peeler or julienne peeler and dragging the cutting edge lengthwise while turning the vegetable. However, most grocery stores now carry spiralized veggies, fresh and frozen, which can save you cupboard space for a tool or the time to spiralize by hand.

Cooking Techniques

Cooking beans. Soak your beans in a bowl of water, preferably overnight. Soaking them first allows the tough, dry shell to soften, which shortens the cooking time and reduces the number of split beans. All beans cook for different amounts of time, based on size and texture, and these times are listed in the recipes. Generally, cooking dried beans takes between 1 and 3 hours and should be done using ample water to cover.

Cooking quinoa. For best results, rinse quinoa well before cooking to remove the natural saponin coating, which can taste bitter or soapy. To wash quinoa, place it in a fine-mesh sieve and rinse under cold water until the water runs clear. To cook, combine the quinoa with twice as much water as the measured quinoa, bring it to a boil, then reduce the heat to a simmer and cook until all liquid has been absorbed. Remove from the heat, cover, and let sit for 5 to 10 minutes to finish cooking.

Dry or water sautéing. It is common to use oil for sautéing veggies such as garlic and onions. However, you can skip the oil in this step. The goal of sautéing is to soften the vegetable cells by heating their internal moisture and, potentially, browning the veggie by cooking out all the moisture. The easiest way to sauté without oil is to have a cup or bottle of water nearby and add it, 1 tablespoon at a time, to avoid cooking too quickly and burning the vegetables.

Soaking nuts. Using raw nuts is a great way to create a whole-food, plant-based cream sauce. Soaking raw nuts before blending or boiling lets their dry, hard outsides soften and allows moisture to be soaked up. The most common nut for a cream sauce is the cashew because it can be pureed smooth and the raw nut has little to no distinct nut flavor.

SPICY SOBA NOODLES WITH
SESAME PEANUT SAUCE ★ PAGE 106

PART TWO

100 WFPB recipes

The recipes in this book are written for the home cook and for those who are new to the whole-food, plant-based diet. Each recipe has been selected to showcase a cooking technique, unique plant ingredient, or a combination of ingredients that will help you become more comfortable creating your own recipes. You'll also see specific labels that highlight attributes of the recipe:

5-INGREDIENT ★ RECIPE USES 5 INGREDIENTS TOTAL

GLUTEN-FREE ★ USES NO GLUTEN-CONTAINING INGREDIENTS

NO COOK ★ RECIPE DOESN'T REQUIRE COOKING

NUT-FREE ★ USE NO NUTS OR NUT BY-PRODUCTS

ONE POT ★ RECIPE ONLY TAKES ONE MAIN PIECE OF EQUIPMENT TO COOK, SUCH AS ONE POT, ONE SKILLET, ONE PAN, OR ONE BAKING DISH

QUICK ★ DISHES THAT CAN BE MADE IN LESS THAN 30 MINUTES

WHOLE WHEAT BLUEBERRY MUFFINS ★ PAGE 50

-3-

BREAKFASTS & SMOOTHIES

TROPICAL GREENS SMOOTHIE

Prep time: 5 minutes ★ **Serves:** 2

GLUTEN-FREE　NO COOK　QUICK

Smoothies start your day with a serving of vegetables. The natural fructose in this smoothie won't cause a midafternoon crash like a sugary baked good, and its 13 grams of fiber help control blood sugar levels. The superfood spirulina contains omega-3 and omega-6 fatty acids and phycocyanin, a powerful antioxidant that can positively affect cholesterol levels.

2 bananas

1 large navel orange, peeled and segmented

1 cup frozen mango chunks

2 cups frozen spinach

2 celery stalks, broken into pieces

2 tablespoons cashew butter or almond butter

1 tablespoon spirulina

1 tablespoon ground flaxseed

1 cup unsweetened nondairy milk, plus more as needed

Water, for thinning (optional)

In a high-speed blender or food processor, combine the bananas, orange, mango, spinach, celery, cashew butter, spirulina (if using), flaxseed, and milk. Blend until creamy, adding more milk or water to thin the smoothie if too thick. Serve immediately—it is best served fresh.

Tip: Buy fresh spinach in bulk for freezing. Wash the spinach well, then lay it out on a clean kitchen towel and pat dry. Store in freezer bags by rolling to compress out the air.

Per Serving (1 smoothie) Calories: 391; Fat: 12g; Protein: 13g; Carbohydrates: 68g; Fiber: 13g

PIÑA COLADA SMOOTHIE BOWL

Prep time: 5 minutes ★ **Serves:** 2

GLUTEN-FREE | NO COOK | QUICK

The iconic piña colada flavor is sweet pineapple combined with creamy milk. Full-fat coconut milk provides a silky mouthfeel and adds a variety of nutritional benefits, but some may question its use because of its high saturated fat levels. Rest assured: A bit of fat is necessary for proper vitamin absorption and brain health. Coconut fat contains lauric acid, which is processed as energy by the liver rather than being stored as fat in the body.

2 bananas, sliced
and frozen

1 cup frozen mango chunks

1 (20-ounce) can pineapple
chunks, drained

1 (14-ounce) can full-fat
coconut milk

1 teaspoon vanilla extract

Water, for thinning
(optional)

Hemp seeds, for garnish

Cashew butter, for garnish

Chia seeds, for garnish
(optional)

Starfruit slices, for garnish
(optional)

Fresh pitted cherries,
for garnish (optional)

1. In a high-speed blender or food processor, combine the bananas, mango, pineapple, coconut milk, and vanilla. Blend until smooth. This smoothie will be thick and may require several starts and stops to scrape the sides down. If it seems too thick, add water to thin.

2. Serve in a bowl topped with hemp seeds, cashew butter, chia seeds starfruit, and cherries (if using). Enjoy as a refreshing drink instead by adding water.

Tip: Slice ripe bananas into ½-inch-thick pieces and freeze them on a sheet of parchment paper before transferring to a freezer bag. Freezing them in small pieces makes blending them faster and easier.

Per Serving (1 smoothie) Calories: 678; Fat: 38g; Protein: 5g; Carbohydrates: 89g; Fiber: 8g

VITAMIN C SMOOTHIE CUBES

Prep time: 5 minutes, plus 8 hours to chill ★ **Makes:** 8 smoothies

`GLUTEN-FREE` `NO COOK` `NUT-FREE`

Vitamin C helps with proper iron absorption and protein metabolism and protects against free radicals. These vitamin C cubes can be added to your smoothie or thawed and thinned with a little water for a naturally sweet breakfast drink.

1 large papaya

1 mango

2 cups chopped pineapple, fresh or frozen

1 cup raw cauliflower florets, fresh or frozen

2 large navel oranges, peeled and halved

1 large orange bell pepper, stemmed, seeded, and coarsely chopped

1. Halve the papaya and mango, remove the pits, and scoop their soft flesh into a high-speed blender.

2. Add the pineapple, cauliflower, oranges, and bell pepper. Blend until smooth.

3. Evenly divide the puree between 2 (16-compartment) ice cube trays and place on a level surface in your freezer. Freeze for at least 8 hours.

4. The cubes can be left in the ice cube trays until use or transferred to a freezer bag. The frozen cubes are good for about 3 weeks in a standard freezer, or up to 6 months in a chest freezer.

Tip: This recipe can be modified in a number of ways. Keep the cauliflower because it is high in vitamin C, but you could swap the papaya for 2 mangos; the orange bell pepper could be omitted or replaced with a red bell pepper; the navel oranges could be replaced with any kind of orange; and peeled grapefruit could be added or used in place of the papaya.

Per Serving (1 smoothie) Calories: 96; Fat: <1g; Protein: 2g; Carbohydrates: 24g; Fiber: 4g

OVERNIGHT CHOCOLATE CHIA PUDDING

Prep time: 2 minutes, plus overnight to chill ⋆ **Serves:** 2

`5-INGREDIENT` `GLUTEN-FREE` `NO COOK`

Chia pudding is easy to make ahead and even doubles for a full week of breakfasts. This no-fuss breakfast is a high-protein, high-fiber option and, when combined with fresh fruit, compotes, and even nut butter, provides a filling way to start your day.

¼ cup chia seeds

1 cup unsweetened nondairy milk

2 tablespoons raw cacao powder

1 teaspoon vanilla extract

1 teaspoon pure maple syrup

1. In a large bowl, stir together the chia seeds, milk, cacao powder, vanilla, and maple syrup. Divide between 2 (½-pint) covered glass jars or containers. Refrigerate overnight.

2. Stir before serving.

Tip: For an easy flavor twist, skip the cacao powder and double the vanilla for a vanilla-flavored pudding. To make a berry pudding, replace the cacao powder with 2 tablespoons of mashed berries, roughly 8 raspberries, to mix in, leave at the bottom, or spoon on top.

Per Serving (1 jar) Calories: 213; Fat: 10g; Protein: 9g; Carbohydrates: 20g; Fiber: 15g

SLOW COOKER SAVORY BUTTERNUT SQUASH OATMEAL

Prep time: 15 minutes ★ **Cook time:** 6 to 8 hours ★ **Serves:** 4

GLUTEN-FREE ONE POT

Oatmeal is a heart-healthy grain rich in soluble fiber and low on the glycemic index, which means it controls blood sugar to help you avoid the midafternoon energy crash you normally get with high-sugar breakfasts. Typically, people associate breakfast oats with sweet flavors, but oats are equally delicious as a savory dish.

1 cup steel-cut oats

2 cups cubed (½-inch pieces) peeled butternut squash (freeze any leftovers after preparing a whole squash for future meals)

3 cups water

¼ cup unsweetened nondairy milk

1 tablespoon chia seeds

2 teaspoons yellow (mellow) miso paste

1½ teaspoons ground ginger

1 tablespoon sesame seeds, toasted

1 tablespoon chopped scallion, green parts only

Shredded carrot, for serving (optional)

1. In a slow cooker, combine the oats, butternut squash, and water.

2. Cover the slow cooker and cook on Low for 6 to 8 hours, or until the squash is fork-tender. Using a potato masher or heavy spoon, roughly mash the cooked butternut squash. Stir to combine with the oats.

3. In a small bowl, whisk together the milk, chia seeds, miso paste, and ginger to combine. Stir the mixture into the oats.

4. Top your oatmeal bowl with sesame seeds and scallion. For more plant-based fiber, top with shredded carrot (if using).

Tip: The long cooking time softens the oats and cooks the butternut squash, but if you're looking for a quicker cooking time, combine everything in a covered stockpot, bring to a simmer, reduce the heat to medium-low, and simmer, stirring occasionally, for 20 minutes.

Per Serving Calories: 230; Fat: 5g; Protein: 7g; Carbohydrates: 40g; Fiber: 9g

CARROT CAKE OATMEAL

Prep time: 10 minutes ★ **Cook time:** 15 minutes ★ **Serves:** 2

GLUTEN-FREE   QUICK

Including shredded carrot in your morning oatmeal boosts nutrition and adds plant-based fiber. The simple combination of familiar spices makes this hearty bowl a decadent treat, and the cinnamon helps curb cravings throughout your morning by controlling blood sugar levels. Top your carrot cake oats with a variety of fresh fruit, nut butters, and seeds to make it even more hearty and nutritious. Quick oats and certified gluten-free oats will give similar results.

¼ cup pecans

1 cup finely shredded carrot

½ cup old-fashioned oats

1¼ cups unsweetened nondairy milk

1 tablespoon pure maple syrup

1 teaspoon ground cinnamon

1 teaspoon ground ginger

¼ teaspoon ground nutmeg

2 tablespoons chia seeds

1. In a small skillet over medium-high heat, toast the pecans for 3 to 4 minutes, stirring often, until browned and fragrant (watch closely, as they can burn quickly). Pour the pecans onto a cutting board and coarsely chop them. Set aside.

2. In an 8-quart pot over medium-high heat, combine the carrot, oats, milk, maple syrup, cinnamon, ginger, and nutmeg. Bring to a boil, then reduce the heat to medium-low. Cook, uncovered, for 10 minutes, stirring occasionally.

3. Stir in the chopped pecans and chia seeds. Serve immediately.

Tip: This oatmeal can also be prepared by mixing all the ingredients in a sealable container and refrigerating overnight. The texture will be more chewy and dense, but overnight oats are an easy way to meal prep for a quick breakfast.

Per Serving Calories: 307; Fat: 17g; Protein: 7g; Carbohydrates: 35g; Fiber: 11g

SPICED SORGHUM & BERRIES

Prep time: 5 minutes ⋆ **Cook time:** about 1 hour ⋆ **Serves:** 4

GLUTEN-FREE ONE POT

There are so many great grains available to us now, and if you're looking for a gluten-free option, try whole-grain sorghum. Sorghum is rich in vitamins and minerals such as B vitamins, phosphorus, magnesium, potassium, iron, and zinc. It is also a good source of fiber and protein. The nuttiness of this grain pairs well with the fresh berries and spices.

1 cup whole-grain sorghum

1 teaspoon ground cinnamon

1 teaspoon Chinese five-spice powder

3 cups water, plus more as needed

1 cup unsweetened nondairy milk

1 teaspoon vanilla extract

2 tablespoons pure maple syrup

1 tablespoon chia seeds

¼ cup sliced almonds

2 cups fresh raspberries, divided

1. In a large pot over medium-high heat, stir together the sorghum, cinnamon, five-spice powder, and water. Bring the water to a boil, cover the pot, and reduce the heat to medium-low. Cook for 1 hour, or until the sorghum is soft and chewy. If the sorghum grains are still hard, add another cup of water and cook for 15 minutes more.

2. In a glass measuring cup, whisk together the milk, vanilla, and maple syrup to blend. Add the mixture to the sorghum, along with the chia seeds, almonds, and 1 cup of raspberries. Gently stir to combine.

3. Serve topped with the remaining 1 cup of fresh raspberries.

Tip: Grains like sorghum can be made ahead and kept refrigerated for up to 1 week. Other grain options for this recipe include buckwheat groats, spelt berries, or barley flakes.

Per Serving Calories: 289; Fat: 8g; Protein: 9g; Carbohydrates: 52g; Fiber: 10g

RAW CINNAMON-APPLE & NUT BOWL

Prep time: 15 minutes, plus 1 hour to chill ★ **Serves:** 4

GLUTEN-FREE   NO COOK

Apples are a good source of vitamin C, fiber, potassium, and a variety of minerals—all essential for healthy digestion. The raw apple helps keep you satisfied longer because its fructose has not been broken down and the fiber hasn't been softened. Use whatever apples you like that are seasonal or on hand but, for a complex flavor, use a firm, sweet apple and a tart apple.

1 green apple, halved, seeded, and cored

3 Honeycrisp apples, halved, seeded, and cored

1 teaspoon freshly squeezed lemon juice

5 pitted Medjool dates

½ teaspoon ground cinnamon

Pinch ground nutmeg

2 tablespoons chia seeds, plus more for serving (optional)

1 tablespoon hemp seeds

¼ cup chopped walnuts

Nut butter, for serving (optional)

1. Finely dice half the green apple and 1 Honeycrisp apple. Store in an airtight container with the lemon juice while you work on next steps.

2. Coarsely chop the remaining apples and the dates. Transfer to a food processor and add the cinnamon and nutmeg. Pulse several times to combine, then process for 2 to 3 minutes to puree. Stir the puree into the reserved diced apples. Stir in the chia seeds (if using), hemp seeds, and walnuts. Refrigerate for at least 1 hour before serving.

3. Serve as is or top with additional chia seeds and nut butter (if using).

Tip: It is tempting to peel the apples before making a dish like this, but the apple skin contains fiber, vitamin C, and ursolic acid, which has been linked to a variety of positive health benefits.

Per Serving Calories: 274; Fat: 8g; Protein: 4g; Carbohydrates: 52g; Fiber: 9g

PEANUT BUTTER & CACAO BREAKFAST QUINOA

Prep time: 5 minutes ★ **Cook time:** 10 minutes ★ **Serves:** 2

GLUTEN-FREE ONE POT QUICK

Quinoa flakes are made in the same way groats are rolled into oats. This process of turning quinoa into flakes makes it faster to cook while keeping all its great nutritional properties like fiber, protein, iron, and B vitamins. Serve your chocolate quinoa with fresh berries, roasted nuts, and a splash of nondairy milk for a hearty and delicious breakfast. Smucker's Natural is a decent brand for the peanut butter.

⅔ cup quinoa flakes

1 cup unsweetened nondairy milk, plus more for serving

1 cup water

¼ cup raw cacao powder

2 tablespoons natural creamy peanut butter

¼ teaspoon ground cinnamon

2 bananas, mashed

Fresh berries of choice, for serving

Chopped nuts of choice, for serving

1. In a 6-quart pot over medium-high heat, stir together the quinoa flakes, milk, water, cacao powder, peanut butter, and cinnamon. Cook, stirring, until the mixture begins to simmer. Turn the heat to medium-low and cook for 3 to 5 minutes, stirring frequently.

2. Stir in the bananas and cook until hot.

3. Serve topped with fresh berries, nuts, and a splash of milk.

Tip: Typically, quinoa takes about 30 minutes to cook. Because they've been pressed, quinoa flakes cook fast, so have all your ingredients ready to go before turning on the heat.

Per Serving Calories: 471; Fat: 16g; Protein: 18g; Carbohydrates: 69g; Fiber: 16g

VANILLA BUCKWHEAT PORRIDGE

Prep time: 5 minutes ★ **Cook time:** 25 minutes ★ **Serves:** 4

GLUTEN-FREE ONE POT QUICK

Buckwheat is an entirely different grain than its name might imply, and it is a good option for those who avoid wheat or gluten. Being very low on the glycemic index, a serving of buckwheat will provide your body with a steady flow of energy throughout the morning. Pair this heart-healthy grain bowl with a serving of nut butter and fresh fruit to satisfy all your morning macronutrient needs.

3 cups water

1 cup raw buckwheat groats

1 teaspoon ground cinnamon

1 banana, sliced

¼ cup golden raisins

¼ cup dried currants

¼ cup sunflower seeds

2 tablespoons chia seeds

1 tablespoon hemp seeds

1 tablespoon sesame seeds, toasted

½ cup unsweetened nondairy milk

1 tablespoon pure maple syrup

1 teaspoon vanilla extract

1. In an 8-quart pot over high heat, bring the water to a boil. Stir in the buckwheat, cinnamon, and banana. Bring the mixture to a boil, stirring, then reduce the heat to medium-low. Cover the pot and cook for 15 minutes, or until the buckwheat is tender. Remove from the heat.

2. Stir in the raisins, currants, sunflower seeds, chia seeds, hemp seeds, sesame seeds, milk, maple syrup, and vanilla. Cover the pot and let sit for 10 minutes before serving.

3. Serve as is or top as desired.

Tip: Buckwheat groats don't soak up water as much as other grains, so the addition of banana and chia seeds helps turn this into a porridge-like consistency. For additional creaminess, add 1 to 2 tablespoons of ground flaxseed.

Per Serving Calories: 353; Fat: 11g; Protein: 10g; Carbohydrates: 61g; Fiber: 10g

POLENTA WITH SEARED PEARS

Prep time: 10 minutes ★ **Cook time:** 50 minutes ★ **Serves:** 4

GLUTEN-FREE   NUT-FREE

Polenta is a cooked cornmeal with roots in a variety of cultures. It can be served as a porridge or chilled for a firm texture that can be sliced, then baked or panfried. This simple recipe has a nutty sweetness from the corn, and the browned pears pair well with the tartness of fresh cranberries.

5¼ cups water, divided, plus more as needed

1½ cups coarse cornmeal

3 tablespoons pure maple syrup

1 tablespoon molasses

1 teaspoon ground cinnamon

2 ripe pears, cored and diced

1 cup fresh cranberries

1 teaspoon chopped fresh rosemary leaves

1. In an 8-quart pot over high heat, bring 5 cups of water to a simmer.

2. While whisking continuously to avoid clumping, slowly pour in the cornmeal. Cook, stirring often with a heavy spoon, for 30 minutes. The polenta should be thick and creamy.

3. While the polenta cooks, in a saucepan over medium heat, stir together the maple syrup, molasses, the remaining ¼ cup of water, and the cinnamon until combined. Bring to a simmer. Add the pears and cranberries. Cook for 10 minutes, stirring occasionally, until the pears are tender and start to brown. Remove from the heat. Stir in the rosemary and let the mixture sit for 5 minutes. If it is too thick, add another ¼ cup of water and return to the heat.

4. Top with the cranberry-pear mixture.

Tip: Look for coarse cornmeal in the bulk food aisle or look for polenta cornmeal with the specialty flours. The canisters of cornmeal are too finely ground for polenta.

Per Serving Calories: 282; Fat: 2g; Protein: 4g; Carbohydrates: 65g; Fiber: 12g

BEST WHOLE WHEAT PANCAKES

Prep time: 10 minutes ★ **Cook time:** 20 minutes ★ **Serves:** 4

QUICK

Most egg-free pancakes rely on bananas or applesauce, but these heavier-binding ingredients make pancakes tough and rubbery. Flaxseed meal, or ground flaxseed, acts as the egg replacer here and adds necessary omega-3 fatty acids. Top your pancakes with date syrup, fresh fruit, and nut butter to make them even more filling and nutritious.

3 tablespoons ground flaxseed

6 tablespoons warm water

1½ cups whole wheat pastry flour

½ cup rye flour

2 tablespoons double-acting baking powder

1 teaspoon ground cinnamon

½ teaspoon ground ginger

1½ cups unsweetened nondairy milk

3 tablespoons pure maple syrup

1 teaspoon vanilla extract

1. In a small bowl, stir together the flaxseed and warm water. Set aside for at least 5 minutes.

2. In a large bowl, whisk together the pastry and rye flours, baking powder, cinnamon, and ginger to combine.

3. In a glass measuring cup, whisk together the milk, maple syrup, and vanilla. Using a spatula, fold the wet ingredients into the dry ingredients. Fold in the soaked flaxseed until fully incorporated.

4. Heat a large skillet or nonstick griddle over medium-high heat. Working in batches, 3 to 4 pancakes at a time, add ¼-cup portions of batter to the hot skillet. Cook for 3 to 4 minutes per side, or until golden brown and no liquid batter is visible.

Tip: Any whole wheat flour will work here, but the best grind for lightly baked goods like this is the pastry variety. Non-pastry grinds have sharper pieces of bran, which can pierce forming air pockets and make your baked goods flat.

Per Serving (3 pancakes) Calories: 301; Fat: 4g; Protein: 10g; Carbohydrates: 57g; Fiber: 10g

SPICED PUMPKIN MUFFINS

Prep time: 15 minutes ★ **Cook time:** 20 minutes ★ **Makes:** 12 muffins

Sneaking vegetables into baked goods boosts fiber, antioxidants, and other vital nutrients. Pumpkin contains high amounts of beta-carotene and potassium—both good for heart health. The warm spices in these muffins complement the natural wheat and pumpkin flavors without being overpowering.

2 tablespoons ground flaxseed

¼ cup water

1¾ cups whole-wheat flour

2 teaspoons baking powder

1½ teaspoons ground cinnamon

½ teaspoon baking soda

½ teaspoon ground ginger

¼ teaspoon ground nutmeg

⅛ teaspoon ground cloves

1 cup pumpkin puree

½ cup pure maple syrup

¼ cup unsweetened applesauce

¼ cup unsweetened nondairy milk

1½ teaspoons vanilla extract

1. Preheat the oven to 350°F. Line a 12-cup metal muffin pan with parchment-paper liners or use a silicone muffin pan.

2. In a small bowl, whisk together the flaxseed and water. Set aside.

3. In a large bowl, whisk together the flour, baking powder, cinnamon, baking soda, ginger, nutmeg, and cloves to combine.

4. In a medium bowl, stir together the pumpkin puree, maple syrup, applesauce, milk, and vanilla. Using a spatula, fold the wet ingredients into the dry ingredients.

5. Fold the soaked flaxseed into the batter until evenly combined, but do not overmix the batter or your muffins will become dense. Spoon about ¼ cup of batter per muffin into your prepared muffin pan.

6. Bake for 18 to 20 minutes, or until a toothpick inserted into the center of a muffin comes out clean. Remove the muffins from the pan and transfer to a wire rack to cool.

7. Store in an airtight container at room temperature for up to 1 week or freeze for up to 3 months.

Tip: When folding wet ingredients into dry ingredients, do not over-mix the batter. The best way to avoid this is to create a well in the dry ingredients, add the wet ingredients, and slowly turn the mixture in on itself using a spatula.

Per Serving (1 muffin) Calories: 115; Fat: 1g; Protein: 3g; Carbohydrates: 25g; Fiber: 3g

WHOLE WHEAT BLUEBERRY MUFFINS

Prep time: 20 minutes ★ **Cook time:** 30 minutes ★ **Makes:** 12 muffins

The lemon zest and earthy spices in these muffins will fill your home with intoxicating aromas. A blend of flours provides nutrients and flavor. Dates and applesauce take the place of sugar and oil.

8 ounces (about 12) Medjool dates, pitted and chopped

1 cup unsweetened nondairy milk

1 tablespoon freshly squeezed lemon juice

1 cup whole wheat flour

½ cup sorghum flour

1 cup millet flour

2 teaspoons baking powder

1 teaspoon ground cinnamon

½ teaspoon ground cardamom

½ teaspoon ground ginger

1 teaspoon lemon zest

½ cup unsweetened applesauce

1 cup fresh or frozen blueberries

½ cup chopped pecans

1. Preheat the oven to 350°F. Line a 12-cup metal muffin pan with parchment-paper liners or use a silicone muffin pan.

2. In a small bowl, stir together the dates, milk, and lemon juice. Set aside.

3. In a medium bowl, whisk together the whole wheat, sorghum, and millet flours; baking powder; cinnamon; cardamom; ginger; and lemon zest to combine.

4. Pour the dates and soaking liquid into a high-speed blender. Blend until smooth. Add the applesauce and blend until combined.

5. Using a heavy spoon, fold the wet ingredients into the dry ingredients. Gently fold in the blueberries and pecans. Spoon about ⅓ cup of batter per muffin into your prepared muffin pan (they should be filled about three-quarters full).

6. Bake for 30 minutes, or until a toothpick inserted into the center of a muffin comes out clean. Let cool in the pan for 15 minutes before removing and transferring to a wire rack to cool.

7. Store in an airtight container at room temperature for up to 1 week or freeze for up to 3 months.

Tip: Muffins made without oil tend to stick to standard cupcake liners. Look for parchment-paper liners at most grocery stores or kitchen supply stores—they will save you a lot of headache. Another option is to use a silicone tray or lightly coat a metal pan with oil.

Per Serving (1 muffin) Calories: 192; Fat: 4g; Protein: 4g; Carbohydrates: 37g; Fiber: 4g

CAULIFLOWER SCRAMBLE

Prep time: 15 minutes ⋆ **Cook time:** 15 minutes ⋆ **Serves:** 4

GLUTEN-FREE QUICK

Start your day with a plate of vegetables and get all the plant-based fiber you need to stay satisfied through the morning. A variety of spices and fresh bell peppers make this scramble a colorful, delicious, and nutritional powerhouse.

1 yellow onion, diced

3 garlic cloves, minced

1 green bell pepper, seeded and coarsely chopped

1 red bell pepper, seeded and coarsely chopped

1 tablespoon water, plus more as needed

1 large cauliflower head, cored, florets coarsely chopped to about ½-inch dice

1 teaspoon ground turmeric

¼ cup nutritional yeast

¼ teaspoon ground nutmeg

¼ teaspoon cayenne pepper

¼ teaspoon freshly ground black pepper

1 tablespoon coconut aminos

1 (15-ounce) can chickpeas, drained and rinsed

1. In a large nonstick skillet over medium heat, combine the onion, garlic, and green and red bell peppers. Cook for 2 to 3 minutes, stirring, until the onion is translucent but not browned. Add the water, 1 tablespoon at a time, to avoid sticking or burning, as needed.

2. Add the cauliflower and toss to combine. Cover the skillet and cook for 5 to 6 minutes, or until the cauliflower is fork-tender.

3. In a small bowl, stir together the turmeric, nutritional yeast, nutmeg, cayenne pepper, and black pepper. Set aside.

4. Evenly sprinkle the coconut aminos over the cauliflower mixture and stir to combine. Stir in the spice mixture. Stir in the chickpeas and cook, uncovered, for 5 minutes to warm.

Tip: Coconut aminos can be used as a gluten-free and lower-sodium substitute for soy sauce in many recipes. The flavor is subtler with a hint of sweetness, but it doesn't taste like coconut.

Per Serving Calories: 243; Fat: 3g; Protein: 18g; Carbohydrates: 40g; Fiber: 14g

VEGGIE BREAKFAST HASH

Prep time: 15 minutes ★ **Cook time:** 25 minutes ★ **Serves:** 4

GLUTEN-FREE   NUT-FREE

This versatile breakfast hash is filling, warming, and easy to prep ahead of time for a quick breakfast. The root vegetables can be mixed and matched to align with seasonal shopping. Enjoy this as a stand-alone breakfast or serve it with fresh greens for a satisfying lunch or dinner.

1 tablespoon dried thyme

2 rosemary sprigs, leaves removed and minced

1 teaspoon Hungarian paprika

½ teaspoon freshly ground black pepper

2 large sweet potatoes, cut into ½-inch cubes

2 parsnips, cut into ½-inch cubes

1 rutabaga, cut into ½-inch cubes

2 Yukon Gold potatoes, cut into ½-inch cubes

4 large carrots, cut into ½-inch cubes

1 large onion, diced

3 garlic cloves, minced

1 (15-ounce) can red kidney beans, drained and rinsed

1 (15-ounce) can chickpeas, drained and rinsed

1. Preheat the oven to 375°F. Line a sheet pan with parchment paper.

2. In a small bowl, stir together the thyme, rosemary, paprika, and pepper. Set aside.

3. Bring a large pot of water to a boil over high heat. Add the sweet potatoes, parsnips, rutabaga, Yukon Gold potatoes, and carrots. Parboil for 2 minutes. Drain well but don't rinse. Transfer to a large bowl. Add the thyme mixture and toss to coat. Spread the parboiled vegetables on the prepared sheet pan and sprinkle with the onion and garlic.

4. Bake for 20 minutes, or until the vegetables are fork-tender.

5. In a medium bowl, stir together the kidney beans and chickpeas. Serve with the cooked vegetable hash.

Tip: Parboiling the root vegetables releases some of their starch, creating a light coating of starch that helps the spices stick and creates a crunchy exterior when baked without using oil.

Per Serving Calories: 458; Fat: 3g; Protein: 17g; Carbohydrates: 94g; Fiber: 20g

ANCIENT GRAINS SALAD ★ PAGE 61

-4-

SALADS & SANDWICHES

RAINBOW COLLARD WRAPS

Prep time: 20 minutes ★ **Serves:** 4

GLUTEN-FREE   NO COOK   QUICK

Full of health benefits like calcium, fiber, iron, and a long list of vitamins, these collard green wraps are visually satisfying as well as easy to make. Plus, your sturdy collard green wraps won't get soggy if you make them ahead.

¼ cup smooth
  peanut butter

2 tablespoons rice vinegar

1 tablespoon
  coconut aminos

1 tablespoon minced
  peeled fresh ginger

½ teaspoon garlic powder

4 large collard green leaves

½ cup hummus

4 carrots, cut into
  matchsticks

1 English cucumber, cut
  into matchsticks

1 red bell pepper, cut into
  thin strips

1 celery stalk, cut into
  thin strips

1 small red cabbage, cut
  into strips

2 avocados, pitted and
  thickly cut

1 cup chopped fresh
  cilantro

1. In a small bowl, whisk together the peanut butter, vinegar, coconut aminos, ginger, and garlic powder to blend. Set aside.

2. Bring an 8-quart pot of water to a boil over high heat. Drop each collard green leaf in the water for 30 seconds. Transfer to a clean kitchen towel and pat dry. Using a sharp kitchen knife, trim the thick, tough rib of each collard green leaf, cutting it so the stem is flush with the rest of the leaf, rather than cutting out the stem completely.

3. Spread 2 tablespoons of hummus down the center of each prepared leaf. Place one-quarter of the carrots, cucumber, bell pepper, celery, red cabbage, and avocados on top of the hummus. Top with a sprinkle of cilantro and a drizzle of peanut butter sauce.

4. Fold each leaf like a burrito, rolling it and folding in the sides to contain the vegetables and filling. Roll the wraps tightly so they are easier to enjoy. Halve and serve.

Per Serving Calories: 378; Fat: 23g; Protein: 11g; Carbohydrates: 37g; Fiber: 14g

CHICKPEA & AVOCADO SALAD

Prep time: 10 minutes ★ **Serves:** 2

GLUTEN-FREE   NO COOK   NUT-FREE   QUICK

This simple salad is a go-to recipe when you're looking for something filling and fresh but you don't want to heat up your house or make a lot of dirty dishes. The fresh flavors in this salad come from the rich creaminess of avocado, the natural sweetness of tomato, and the refreshing coolness of cucumber. You can use a variety of leafy greens for this salad to add both bulk and crispness.

1 cup chopped romaine lettuce

1 cup arugula

1 (15-ounce) can chickpeas, drained and rinsed

1 cup diced (½-inch) English cucumber

1 cup cherry tomatoes, halved

1 large avocado, halved, pitted, and diced

1 teaspoon dried parsley

½ teaspoon dried thyme

Freshly ground black pepper

3 tablespoons apple cider vinegar

1. In a large bowl, toss together the romaine lettuce, arugula, chickpeas, cucumber, tomatoes, avocado, parsley, and thyme. Season with pepper.

2. Sprinkle on the vinegar and toss to coat.

3. This salad is best enjoyed fresh but can be refrigerated to serve the following day.

Tip: You can use a standard cucumber for this recipe but English cucumbers are less watery and their skin is thinner, so you can skip the peeling.

Per Serving Calories: 380; Fat: 19g; Protein: 13g; Carbohydrates: 45g; Fiber: 18g

WARM SWEET POTATO & BRUSSELS SPROUT SALAD

Prep time: 20 minutes ★ **Cook time:** 30 minutes ★ **Serves:** 4

GLUTEN-FREE

This salad is a comforting combination of flavors and textures. The roasted sweet potato is earthy with a natural caramel flavor, which is a pleasant contrast to the crispness of the raw Brussels sprouts. A splash of balsamic vinegar along with walnuts and dried cranberries bring it all together.

3 sweet potatoes, peeled and cut into ¼-inch dice

1 teaspoon dried thyme

1 teaspoon garlic powder

½ teaspoon onion powder

1 pound Brussels sprouts

1 cup walnuts, chopped

¼ cup reduced-sugar dried cranberries

2 tablespoons balsamic vinegar

Freshly ground black pepper

1. Preheat the oven to 450°F. Line a baking sheet with parchment paper.

2. Place the sweet potatoes in a colander and rinse. Shake the colander to remove excess water. Sprinkle the damp sweet potatoes with the thyme, garlic powder, and onion powder. Toss to coat evenly with the spices. Transfer to the prepared baking sheet and spread the sweet potatoes in a single layer.

3. Bake for 20 minutes. Flip the sweet potatoes and bake for 10 minutes more, until fork-tender.

4. While the sweet potatoes roast, wash the Brussels sprouts and remove any tough or discolored outer leaves. Using a large chef's knife, halve the Brussels lengthwise. Place them cut-side down and thinly slice the sprouts crosswise into thin shreds. Discard the root end and loosen the shreds.

5. In a large bowl, toss together the Brussels sprouts, sweet potatoes, walnuts, and cranberries. Drizzle with the vinegar and season with pepper.

Tip: A balsamic reduction works even better for this recipe. Make your own by simmering 1 cup of balsamic vinegar over low heat for 20 to 30 minutes, or until it thickens and reduces by half. Refrigerate for up to 1 month.

Per Serving Calories: 360; Fat: 20g; Protein: 10g; Carbohydrates: 44g; Fiber: 12g

MASHED CHICKPEA SANDWICH

Prep time: 10 minutes ★ **Serves:** 4

`NO COOK` `NUT-FREE` `QUICK`

There is nothing more iconic than the picnic classic egg salad sandwich. If you're looking to enjoy the same ease of creation and combination of flavors, this chickpea sandwich takes only minutes to prepare and uses plant-based ingredients to create a creamy and flavorful sandwich spread. The avocado adds heart-healthy fats, lutein, and beta-carotene, and is a good source of potassium.

1 large ripe avocado, halved and pitted

1 (15-ounce) can chickpeas, drained and rinsed

¼ cup diced sweet pickle, or relish (optional)

¼ cup diced red onion

1 celery stalk, diced

1 teaspoon Dijon mustard

1 teaspoon dried dill

½ teaspoon garlic powder

Whole-grain bread, pita, or romaine lettuce leaves, for serving

1. Scoop the avocado flesh into a medium bowl. Using a potato masher or a heavy spoon, mash the avocado until smooth.

2. Add the chickpeas and mash lightly so some larger pieces of chickpea remain for texture.

3. Using a spoon or spatula, mix in the pickle (if using), red onion, celery, mustard, dill, and garlic powder. Serve immediately on bread or lettuce leaves or refrigerate overnight for an even more blended flavor.

Tip: Replace the avocado with ¼ cup of tahini. The texture will still be creamy, but your chickpea spread will have a slightly nutty flavor.

Per Serving Calories: 182; Fat: 9g; Protein: 6g; Carbohydrates: 21g; Fiber: 8g

ANCIENT GRAINS SALAD

Prep time: 20 minutes ★ **Cook time:** 55 minutes ★ **Serves:** 6

NUT-FREE

Ancient grains are making their way back into kitchens because of their nutritional benefits and flavor. Farro is nutty tasting and cooks to a chewy texture. Rye berries are nutrient dense and have a high level of magnesium, which helps stabilize the body's glucose absorption. Both grains offer a high amount of soluble fiber, which aids digestion and blood sugar levels.

¼ cup farro

¼ cup raw rye berries

2 ripe pears, cored and coarsely chopped

2 celery stalks, coarsely chopped

1 green apple, cored and coarsely chopped

½ cup chopped fresh parsley

¼ cup golden raisins

3 tablespoons freshly squeezed lemon juice

¼ teaspoon ground cumin

Pinch cayenne pepper

1. In an 8-quart pot, combine the farro, rye berries, and enough water to cover by 3 inches. Bring to a boil over high heat. Reduce the heat to medium-low, cover the pot, and cook for 45 to 50 minutes, or until the grains are firm and chewy but not hard. Drain and set aside to cool.

2. In a large bowl, gently stir together the cooled grains, pears, celery, apple, parsley, raisins, lemon juice, cumin, and cayenne pepper. Serve immediately or refrigerate in an airtight container for up to 1 week.

Tip: Many grains are suitable for this recipe. The goal is to use whole grains, like farro, rye, wheat berries, or kamut, to get the most fiber and mineral benefits from the full grain. You can also cook the grains ahead to make a weekday meal even easier.

Per Serving Calories: 127; Fat: 1g; Protein: 3g; Carbohydrates: 31g; Fiber: 5g

KALE, BLACK BEAN & QUINOA SALAD

Prep time: 20 minutes * **Cook time:** 30 minutes, plus 1 hour to chill * **Serves:** 6

GLUTEN-FREE · ONE POT

This vibrant, nutrient-dense salad is great for a potluck or as a side dish for dinner. The cooked and chilled quinoa is chewy with some crunch and is a complete protein that adds fiber to your meal. Kale's earthiness is brightened with a splash of lemon and cumin. This dish gets better with age, so I recommend making it at least a day before serving.

2 garlic cloves,
  finely minced

½ yellow onion, diced

2 tablespoons water

2¼ cups no-sodium
  vegetable broth, divided

1 cup dried tricolor
  quinoa, rinsed

1 tablespoon freshly
  squeezed lemon juice

1 teaspoon lemon zest

1 teaspoon chia seeds

1 teaspoon smoked ancho
  chili powder

1 teaspoon ground cumin

6 cups chopped kale leaves

1 (15-ounce) can black
  beans, drained and rinsed

1 carrot, grated

1 red bell pepper, diced

1. In an 8-quart pot over medium-high heat, combine the garlic, onion, and water. Sauté for 2 to 3 minutes, or until the water evaporates. Add 2 cups of vegetable broth and the quinoa. Bring to a simmer, stirring, then reduce the heat to medium-low, cover the pot, and cook for 20 minutes. The quinoa is done when the grain has a translucent center with a distinct ring around the edge and, when tested, is chewy, not hard. Remove from the heat and let cool.

2. While the quinoa cooks, in a glass measuring cup, whisk together the remaining ¼ cup of vegetable broth, the lemon juice, lemon zest, chia seeds, ancho chili powder, and cumin to blend. Let stand for 5 minutes to let the chia seeds soak and the sauce thicken.

3. Place the kale in a large bowl. Pour in half the dressing, reserving half for serving. Using your hands, squeeze together the kale and dressing to soften the kale. If you want even more tender kale, steam or blanch it before adding the dressing.

4. Stir in the quinoa, black beans, carrot, and bell pepper. Refrigerate for at least 1 hour before serving or, for best results, up to 1 day. Serve with the reserved dressing.

Tip: It may seem strange to massage your vegetables, but your hands are capable of softening kale leaves better than a spoon. The lemon juice and liquid in the dressing help break down the tough kale leaves.

Per Serving Calories: 207; Fat: 3g; Protein: 10g; Carbohydrates: 37g; Fiber: 10g

CURRIED KALE SLAW

Prep time: 20 minutes ★ **Serves:** 4

`GLUTEN-FREE` `NO COOK` `QUICK`

Fresh kale provides a calcium and fiber boost and curry spices contribute a unique twist to this traditional side dish. The apple in the slaw adds fiber as well as sweetness that pairs well with the earthy kale and curry flavors.

For the dressing

⅔ cup water

2 tablespoons apple cider vinegar

2 tablespoons pure maple syrup

1 garlic clove, minced

1 teaspoon grated peeled fresh ginger

1 teaspoon Dijon mustard

½ teaspoon curry powder

Freshly ground black pepper

For the slaw

1 apple, shredded

1 tablespoon freshly squeezed lemon juice

3 cups thinly sliced kale

1 carrot, shredded

1 cup shredded fennel

¼ cup golden raisins

¼ cup sliced almonds, plus more for garnish

To make the dressing

1. In a blender, combine the water, vinegar, maple syrup, garlic, ginger, mustard, and curry powder. Season with pepper. Puree until smooth. Set aside.

To make the slaw

2. In a large bowl, toss together the apple and lemon juice.

3. Add the kale, carrot, fennel, raisins, and almonds and toss to combine the slaw ingredients.

4. Add about three-quarters of the dressing and toss to coat. Taste and add more dressing as needed. Let sit for 10 minutes to allow the kale leaves to soften. Toss again and top with additional sliced almonds to serve.

Tip: You can use a whisk to make the dressing but it emulsifies better and faster using a blender.

Per Serving Calories: 147; Fat: 4g; Protein: 3g; Carbohydrates: 26g; Fiber: 4g

PESTO POTATO SALAD

Prep time: 15 minutes ★ **Cook time:** 20 minutes ★ **Serves:** 4

GLUTEN-FREE

Potato salad often relies on eggs or a heavy vinegar sauce for flavor. This recipe builds flavor with an oil-free pesto, roasted red potatoes, and peppery greens and radishes. The natural oils in walnuts create a smooth, creamy pesto loaded with healthy fats and nutrients.

1 pound red potatoes,
washed and patted dry

2 tablespoons Everyday
Pesto (page 164)

2 cups arugula

1 cup radish matchsticks

1 cup watercress

1 celery stalk, diced

Freshly ground
black pepper

1. Preheat the oven to 425°F. Line a baking sheet with parchment paper.

2. Halve the potatoes, or quarter them if larger. Place potatoes, cut-side down, on the prepared baking sheet.

3. Bake for 15 minutes. Flip the potatoes and bake for 5 more minutes, until fork-tender. Remove and let cool.

4. In a large bowl, toss together the cooled potatoes and 2 tablespoons of pesto. Add the arugula, radish, watercress, celery, and 1 more tablespoon of pesto. Toss to combine and coat. Season with pepper.

Per Serving Calories: 290; Fat: 17g; Protein: 11g; Carbohydrates: 28g; Fiber: 7g

SOUTHWESTERN BLACK BEAN PASTA SALAD

Prep time: 15 minutes ★ **Cook time:** 15 minutes, plus 1 hour to chill ★ **Serves:** 4

NUT-FREE

Pasta salad is an easy meal or side dish for a beginner cook to master. This nutrient-dense salad is a combination of bold flavors coming from fresh peppers and a rich, creamy sauce made with blended avocado and spices. This recipe is simple to double for a picnic, potluck, or office party and stores well in the refrigerator for meal prep.

8 ounces whole wheat rotini pasta

1 large avocado, halved and pitted

2 tablespoons freshly squeezed lime juice

1½ teaspoons chili powder

1 teaspoon smoked paprika

1 teaspoon ground cumin

1 garlic clove, chopped

1 (15-ounce) can corn, drained

1 (15-ounce) black beans, drained and rinsed

1 small red bell pepper, diced

1 pint cherry tomatoes, halved

¼ cup chopped red onion

½ cup chopped fresh cilantro

1. Cook the pasta according to package instructions. Drain, rinse lightly, and let cool.

2. Scoop the avocado flesh into a blender and add the lime juice, chili powder, paprika, cumin, and garlic. Blend until smooth.

3. In a large bowl, toss together the pasta, corn, black beans, bell pepper, tomatoes, red onion, cilantro, and dressing until well mixed. Refrigerate for at least 1 hour before serving or, for best results, up to 1 day.

Tip: The pasta can be replaced with a spiralized vegetable like carrot or zucchini. The sauce also works well on a hearty whole grain like farro or kamut.

Per Serving Calories: 478; Fat: 10g; Protein: 18g; Carbohydrates: 84g; Fiber: 17g

RAW CARROT & DATE WALNUT SALAD

Prep time: 15 minutes ★ **Serves:** 4 to 6

GLUTEN-FREE   NO COOK   QUICK

Vibrantly colored with a pleasant combination of sweetness, a little heat, and citrus, this easy salad is a perfect side for a hearty meal or can be enjoyed as a stand-alone main. The dates contribute a caramel-like flavor that pairs well with the umami from the walnuts and mustard.

2 tablespoons apple
  cider vinegar

¼ cup water

1 teaspoon Dijon mustard

1 tablespoon lemon zest

1 tablespoon pure
  maple syrup

¼ teaspoon freshly ground
  black pepper

½ teaspoon
  cayenne pepper

10 carrots

1 small red onion

4 dates, finely chopped

¼ cup golden raisins

½ cup walnuts, chopped

1. In a small bowl, whisk together the vinegar, water, mustard, lemon zest, maple syrup, black pepper, and cayenne pepper to combine. Set aside.

2. Using a mandoline, cut the carrots and red onion with the julienne blade. Transfer to a large bowl and add the dates, raisins, and walnuts. Toss to combine.

3. Pour in the dressing and toss until fully incorporated. Serve immediately or refrigerate in an airtight container overnight.

Tip: The julienne cut is the perfect size for this salad but if you don't have a mandoline, cut the carrots and onion to matchstick size by hand or shred using a box grater.

Per Serving Calories: 229; Fat: 10g; Protein: 4g; Carbohydrates: 34g; Fiber: 6g

CHICKPEA GYROS

Prep time: 15 minutes ⋆ **Cook time:** 20 minutes ⋆ **Serves:** 4

NUT-FREE

These chickpea gyros are full of rich flavors and aromas using standard pantry spices. The crisp texture and earthy seasoning of the roasted chickpeas pair well with fresh cucumber and tomato.

1 tablespoon paprika

1 teaspoon freshly ground black pepper

1 teaspoon dried oregano

½ teaspoon garlic powder

¼ teaspoon cayenne pepper

¼ teaspoon onion powder

1 (15-ounce) can chickpeas, drained and rinsed

1 cup hummus

4 whole wheat pitas

¼ cup finely chopped cucumber

¼ cup red onion strips

¼ cup chopped tomato

2 romaine lettuce leaves, finely chopped

1. Preheat the oven to 400°F. Line a baking sheet with parchment paper.

2. In a medium bowl, stir together the paprika, black pepper, oregano, garlic powder, cayenne pepper, and onion powder. Add the chickpeas and toss to coat. Spread the chickpeas into a single layer on the prepared baking sheet.

3. Bake for 10 minutes. Stir and flip the chickpeas and bake for 10 minutes more, until slightly crispy (they will become crispier as they cool). Remove from the oven and let cool on the baking sheet.

4. Spread ¼ cup of hummus on each pita. Top each with one-quarter of the roasted chickpeas, 1 tablespoon each of the cucumber, red onion, and tomato, and one-quarter of the lettuce. Fold and enjoy.

Tip: Keeping the chickpeas a little damp will help the spices stick to them. If you want them crispier, pat the chickpeas dry then lightly spray with oil before tossing in the spices.

Per Serving Calories: 400; Fat: 11g; Protein: 15g; Carbohydrates: 61g; Fiber: 13g

TABBOULEH

Prep time: 20 minutes ★ **Cook time:** 15 minutes ★ **Serves:** 4

NUT-FREE

Tabbouleh is a fresh mixture of herbs and bulgur and is a mainstay in the whole-food, plant-based diet. It is loaded with flavors and nutrients from tomatoes, olives, and cucumber. Bulgur is made from cracked wheat and is a heart-healthy grain with 30 percent of your daily recommended fiber in a single serving. This Middle Eastern-inspired dish is easy to make ahead for a filling lunch or side.

½ cup bulgur

2 bunches fresh parsley, finely chopped

2 Roma tomatoes, diced

1 cup diced English cucumber

1 small red bell pepper, diced

½ cup finely chopped scallions, green parts only

¼ cup green olives, pitted and coarsely chopped

¼ cup chopped fresh mint

¼ cup freshly squeezed lemon juice

1 garlic clove, minced

1. Soak or cook the bulgur according to the package instructions. Drain.

2. In a large bowl, combine the bulgur, parsley, tomatoes, cucumber, bell pepper, scallions, olives, mint, lemon juice, and garlic. Gently mix until completely combined. Let rest for 15 minutes before serving or refrigerate overnight in an airtight container.

Tip: Tabbouleh can be modified in a number of ways for taste preferences. You can omit the mint, but it does give the dish a freshness that pairs well with the cucumber and red pepper.

Per Serving Calories: 107; Fat: 2g; Protein: 4g; Carbohydrates: 21g; Fiber: 5g

GRILLED ZUCCHINI & HUMMUS WRAP

Prep time: 15 minutes ★ **Cook time:** 6 minutes ★ **Serves:** 2

NUT-FREE   QUICK

This recipe is extremely versatile. Veggies can be swapped based on preference. If you don't like kale, use fresh spinach or even romaine lettuce. The zucchini can be grilled ahead and the veggies can be prepared in advance to make this a quick and easy lunch option. Use a plain hummus or Creamy Roasted Red Pepper Hummus (page 154) for even more flavor.

1 zucchini, ends removed, thinly sliced lengthwise

½ teaspoon dried oregano

¼ teaspoon freshly ground black pepper

¼ teaspoon garlic powder

¼ cup hummus

2 whole wheat tortillas

2 Roma tomatoes, cut lengthwise into slices

1 cup chopped kale

2 tablespoons chopped red onion

½ teaspoon ground cumin

1. In a skillet over medium heat, place the zucchini slices and cook for 3 minutes per side. Sprinkle with the oregano, pepper, and garlic powder and remove from the heat.

2. Spread 2 tablespoons of hummus on each tortilla. Lay half the zucchini in the center of each tortilla. Top with tomato slices, kale, red onion, and ¼ teaspoon of cumin. Wrap tightly and enjoy.

Tip: When selecting zucchini for a recipe like this, choose one that is thin and firm. A large zucchini will have too much moisture and not cook as firmly.

Per Serving Calories: 247; Fat: 8g; Protein: 9g; Carbohydrates: 37g; Fiber: 8g

GREEN GODDESS SANDWICH

Prep time: 20 minutes, plus 1 hour to chill ★ **Serves:** 2

NO COOK   NUT-FREE

Green goddess spread is vibrant and full of fresh flavors. Typically, this spread or dressing is made with mayonnaise, but using a soft bean makes this creamy, oil-free, and fiber-rich.

For the spread

1 (15-ounce) can cannellini beans, drained and rinsed

⅓ cup packed fresh basil leaves

⅓ cup packed fresh parsley

⅓ cup chopped fresh chives

2 garlic cloves, chopped

Zest and juice of ½ lemon

1 tablespoon apple cider vinegar

For the sandwiches

4 whole-grain bread slices, toasted

8 English cucumber slices

1 large beefsteak tomato, cut into slices

1 large avocado, halved, pitted, and cut into slices

1 small yellow bell pepper, cut into slices

2 handfuls broccoli sprouts

2 handfuls fresh spinach

To make the spread

1. In a food processor, combine the cannellini beans, basil, parsley, chives, garlic, lemon zest and juice, and vinegar. Pulse a few times, scrape down the sides, and puree until smooth. You may need to scrape down the sides again to incorporate all the basil and parsley. Refrigerate for at least 1 hour to allow the flavors to blend.

To assemble the sandwiches

2. Build your sandwiches by spreading several tablespoons of green goddess spread on each slice of bread. Layer two slices of bread with the cucumber, tomato, avocado, bell pepper, broccoli sprouts, and spinach. Top with the remaining bread slices and press down lightly.

Tip: Cannellini beans make this a creamy spread, but you can also use chickpeas, pinto beans, or great northern beans. You can also replace the beans with avocado.

Per Serving Calories: 619; Fat: 21g; Protein: 28g; Carbohydrates: 86g; Fiber: 26g

TEX-MEX QUINOA
VEGETABLE SOUP *
PAGE 90

-5-

SOUPS & STEWS

HUNGARIAN RED LENTIL SOUP

Prep time: 10 minutes ★ **Cook time:** 25 minutes ★ **Serves:** 4

GLUTEN-FREE ONE POT

Soup is one of the meals to master first because it teaches you about knife use, flavor combinations, and seasoning. This red lentil soup gets its name from Hungarian paprika, which is mildly sweeter than its Spanish counterpart.

1 large yellow onion, diced

3 garlic cloves, minced

3 cups water, plus
1 tablespoon and more
as needed

4 ounces tomato paste

2 tablespoons Hungarian
paprika, plus more for
seasoning

1 teaspoon ground mustard

¼ teaspoon freshly ground
black pepper, plus more
for seasoning

3 carrots, diced

1 celery stalk, diced

1 cup dried red
lentils, rinsed

1 (14-ounce) can light
coconut milk

Chopped scallions, green
parts only, for serving

1. In an 8-quart pot over high heat, combine the onion and garlic. Sauté for 2 to 3 minutes, adding water, 1 tablespoon at a time, to prevent burning, until the onion is translucent but not browned.

2. Add the tomato paste, paprika, mustard, and pepper. Cook, stirring, for 2 minutes.

3. Stir in the remaining 3 cups of water. Add the carrots and celery. Bring the soup to a simmer and add the lentils. Reduce the heat to medium-low, cover the pot, and cook for 10 minutes.

4. Stir in the coconut milk and bring the mixture to a simmer, stirring continuously. Cook for 5 minutes, or until the lentils are tender.

5. Serve topped with scallions and a sprinkle of Hungarian paprika and pepper.

Tip: Use sweet Hungarian paprika, not the hot variety—the hot version is labeled as such, whereas the sweet might just be called "Hungarian." Light coconut milk provides a more subtle flavor than the full-fat variety.

Per Serving Calories: 309; Fat: 9g; Protein: 15g; Carbohydrates: 48g; Fiber: 10g

SPINACH, BARLEY & CARROT SOUP

Prep time: 10 minutes ★ **Cook time:** 25 minutes ★ **Serves:** 4

NUT-FREE ONE POT

This recipe has three main components: Spinach is high in iron, calcium, and a variety of phytonutrients. Barley is a good source of fiber and B vitamins such as thiamine, riboflavin, and niacin. Carrots are high in beta-carotene, fiber, and necessary vitamins and minerals. Customize this recipe using another leafy green or a gluten-free grain like spelt.

6 multicolored carrots, cut into 1-inch pieces

½ cup barley

1 (15-ounce) can diced tomatoes

2 garlic cloves, minced

4 cups no-sodium vegetable broth

2 cups water

4 cups fresh spinach

¼ cup chopped fresh basil leaves, plus more for garnish

2 tablespoons chopped fresh chives, plus more for garnish

1 (15-ounce) can cannellini beans, rinsed and drained

1 tablespoon balsamic vinegar

Freshly ground black pepper

1. In a large pot over medium heat, combine the carrots, barley, tomatoes with their juices, garlic, vegetable broth, and water. Bring to a simmer. Cover the pot and cook for 10 minutes, or until the barley is chewy and not hard.

2. Place spinach, basil, and chives on top of the water but do not stir. Cover the pot, reduce heat to low, and cook for 3 minutes to soften the leaves.

3. Stir the pot and add the cannellini beans and vinegar. Remove the pot from the heat and let sit, covered, for 5 minutes. Garnish with chives, basil, and a pinch of pepper to serve.

Tip: You can steam the leaves of whatever green you're using ahead of time or use a steamer insert for your pot if you have one, but cooking them over low heat while floating them on the soup works well.

Per Serving Calories: 261; Fat: 2g; Protein: 12g; Carbohydrates: 50g; Fiber: 14g

WILD RICE MUSHROOM SOUP

Prep time: 15 minutes, plus 1 hour to soak ★ Cook time: 45 minutes ★ Serves: 4

Using a combination of rice gives this soup texture, flavor, and a variety of nutritional benefits. The fresh herbs bring this soup to life, and the walnuts soaked in the stock take the place of butter and add antioxidants and omega-3 fatty acids. This soup will soon become a cool-weather favorite.

4 cups no-sodium vegetable broth

½ cup walnuts

9 ounces baby portabella mushrooms, coarsely chopped

4 ounces shiitake mushrooms, coarsely chopped

1 tablespoon balsamic vinegar, plus more for drizzling

4 garlic cloves, minced

½ celery stalk, minced

3 thyme sprigs, divided

3 tablespoons whole wheat flour

4 cups unsweetened nondairy milk

½ cup wild rice

½ cup brown rice

1 rosemary sprig

Freshly ground black pepper

1. In a high-speed blender, combine the vegetable broth and walnuts. Let sit for 1 hour to soften the walnuts. You can also soak the walnuts overnight in an airtight glass container.

2. In an 8-quart pot over medium-high heat, combine the portabella and shiitake mushrooms. Cook for 5 minutes to expel most of the liquid from the mushrooms. Pour on the vinegar and cook for 1 minute more. Turn off the heat. Transfer the mushrooms to a non-plastic bowl.

3. Transfer ¼ cup of the mushroom mixture to the blender with the vegetable broth and walnuts. Blend until the mushrooms and walnuts are fully incorporated. Set aside.

4. Place the empty pot over medium-high heat and combine the garlic, celery, and 1 thyme sprig. Sauté for 1 minute.

5. Add the mushrooms back to the pot. Add the flour and stir to coat the mushrooms.

6. Pour in the blended stock and add the milk, wild and brown rice, rosemary sprig, and remaining 2 thyme sprigs. Bring the mixture to a simmer, turn the heat to medium-low, cover the pot, and cook for 25 to 30 minutes, or until the rice is tender but chewy.

7. Season with pepper and a drizzle of vinegar.

Tip: This soup is best enjoyed immediately. The longer the rice sits, the softer it will become, rather than staying firm as intended. You can add more liquid to serve if you will be eating it after refrigeration.

Per Serving Calories: 337; Fat: 12g; Protein: 12g; Carbohydrates: 51g; Fiber: 6g

SPICY CAULIFLOWER & CARROT GINGER SOUP

Prep time: 15 minutes ★ **Cook time:** 55 minutes ★ **Serves:** 6

GLUTEN-FREE

The flavor in this soup is built by roasting the vegetables. Roasting adds richness by caramelizing the natural sugars in the vegetables. The soup has a pleasant kick from the curry powder and red pepper flakes, but it's not so spicy that it'll distract from the vegetables. You can prep ahead, roasting the vegetables and refrigerating them days before making the soup.

6 carrots, coarsely chopped

1 cauliflower head, cut into florets

1 sweet potato, peeled and chopped

1 yellow onion, coarsely chopped

2 garlic cloves, minced

1 tablespoon water, plus more as needed

1 tablespoon minced peeled fresh ginger

1 teaspoon red pepper flakes

6 cups no-sodium vegetable broth

1 (14-ounce) can full-fat coconut milk

1 tablespoon freshly squeezed lemon juice

1. Preheat the oven to 450°F. Line a baking sheet with parchment paper.

2. Spread the carrots, cauliflower, and sweet potato evenly on the prepared baking sheet.

3. Bake for 30 minutes. Flip the vegetables and bake for 10 minutes more, until lightly browned and fork-tender.

4. In an 8-quart pot over high heat, combine the onion and garlic. Sauté for 2 to 3 minutes, adding water, 1 tablespoon at a time, to prevent burning, until the onion is translucent but not browned. Add the ginger and red pepper flakes and cook for 1 minute more.

5. Pour in the vegetable broth and bring the soup to a boil.

6. Add the roasted vegetables and bring the soup to simmer. Cover the pot and cook for 5 minutes.

1 tablespoon yellow
curry powder

2 teaspoons ground
turmeric

½ cup coarsely chopped
fresh cilantro

Pumpkin seeds, for serving

Cayenne pepper, for
seasoning

7. Add the coconut milk, lemon juice, curry powder, and turmeric. Using an immersion blender, puree until smooth. Stir in the cilantro.

8. Top with pumpkin seeds and a sprinkle of cayenne pepper.

Tip: Using an immersion blender for a large pot of soup like this avoids the potential kitchen mess of using a standard blender. It also saves time, because you don't need to transfer the soup in stages.

Per Serving Calories: 213; Fat: 13g; Protein: 5g; Carbohydrates: 23g; Fiber: 6g

ROASTED POTATO & CAULIFLOWER SOUP

Prep time: 20 minutes ★ **Cook time:** 30 minutes ★ **Serves:** 6

Cauliflower is a great base for soups because it purees smoothly and contains some of almost every vitamin and mineral you need. Cauliflower is also high in fiber and a variety of cancer-fighting antioxidants, such as glucosinolates and isothiocyanates. This soup is an earthy blend of roasted cauliflower and russet potatoes, enhanced with fresh rosemary and thyme. The soup's creaminess comes from the starch of potato, and salt is replaced using herbs, spices, and other plant-based ingredients.

8 garlic cloves, peeled

1 large cauliflower head, cut into small florets

2 russet potatoes, peeled and chopped into 1-inch pieces

1 yellow onion, coarsely chopped

1 celery stalk, coarsely chopped

1 tablespoon water, plus more as needed

6 cups no-sodium vegetable broth

2 thyme sprigs

2 teaspoons paprika

¼ teaspoon freshly ground black pepper

1 tablespoon chopped fresh rosemary leaves

1. Preheat the oven to 450°F. Line a baking sheet with parchment paper.

2. Wrap the garlic cloves in aluminum foil or place in a garlic roaster.

3. Evenly spread the cauliflower and potatoes on the prepared baking sheet. Place the wrapped garlic on the baking sheet.

4. Roast for 15 to 20 minutes, or until the cauliflower is lightly browned.

5. In an 8-quart pot over high heat, combine the onion and celery. Sauté for 4 to 5 minutes, adding water, 1 tablespoon at a time, to prevent burning, until the onion starts to brown.

6. Pour in the vegetable broth and bring the soup to a simmer.

7. Add the roasted vegetables and garlic, thyme, paprika, and pepper. Bring the soup to a simmer, cover the pot, and cook for 10 minutes.

8. Remove and discard the thyme. Using an immersion blender, puree the soup until smooth. If the soup is too thick, add water, as needed, to the desired consistency.

9. Stir in the rosemary.

Tip: This is another great soup to prep ahead of time by roasting the vegetables, then refrigerating them in an airtight container for a quick weekday meal.

Per Serving Calories: 120; Fat: 1g; Protein: 5g; Carbohydrates: 26g; Fiber: 5g

MOROCCAN-INSPIRED CHICKPEA STEW

Prep time: 20 minutes ★ **Cook time:** 30 minutes ★ **Serves:** 4

GLUTEN-FREE NUT-FREE ONE POT

This stew's flavor is less about the ingredients and more about the cooking process. By slowly browning the onions and garlic and cooking the spices, a deep, rich flavor emerges. The earthiness of cumin and the browned onions is balanced with the sweet flavors of tomato and brightness of cilantro and lime. Serve with crusty whole wheat bread for dipping, or a scoop of couscous.

1 tablespoon Hungarian paprika

1 teaspoon smoked paprika

1 teaspoon ground cumin

1 teaspoon onion powder

1 large yellow onion, coarsely chopped

4 garlic cloves, diced

1 tablespoon water, plus more as needed

2 carrots, diced

1 tablespoon pure maple syrup

1 (28-ounce) can crushed tomatoes

½ cup packed chopped fresh cilantro

1 (15-ounce) can chickpeas, drained and rinsed

1 (15-ounce) dark red kidney beans, drained and rinsed

Juice of ½ lime

1. In a small bowl, stir together the Hungarian paprika, smoked paprika, cumin, and onion powder. Set aside.

2. In an 8-quart pot over high heat, combine the onion, garlic, and 1 tablespoon of water. Turn the heat to medium-low. Cook for at least 10 minutes, stirring occasionally. Add more water, 1 tablespoon at a time, to prevent burning, until the onion is deeply browned.

3. Stir in the carrots. Turn the heat to high.

4. Stir in the paprika mixture and cook for 30 seconds, stirring continuously to prevent burning. Pour in the maple syrup and cook for 30 seconds more, stirring.

5. Carefully pour in the tomatoes with their juices. To avoid splatter, pour the tomatoes onto a spoon and not directly into the hot pot. Bring to a simmer, stirring, then turn the heat to low, cover the pot, and cook for 10 minutes.

6. Stir in the cilantro, chickpeas, and kidney beans. Cover the pot and cook for 5 minutes more to warm.

7. Sprinkle with lime juice before serving.

8. Enjoy this stew as is or top as desired. I like coarsely chopped cilantro leaves, scallion greens, and jalapeño pepper.

Tip: Cooking your spices for 15 to 30 seconds before adding the liquids can bring out their complex flavors. The key to avoid scorching is to stir continuously and have your liquid ready to add immediately to stop the cooking process.

Per Serving Calories: 331; Fat: 3g; Protein: 17g; Carbohydrates: 65g; Fiber: 15g

CURRIED ACORN SQUASH SOUP

Prep time: 20 minutes ★ **Cook time:** about 1 hour ★ **Serves:** 6

This creamy soup is a unique blend of naturally sweet squash and complex curry flavors. The health benefits of acorn squash are worth the little bit of prep it takes. Acorn squash is high in vitamin C, potassium, magnesium, and fiber, and is an excellent source of B vitamins. You can enjoy this soup as a creamy side dish or bulk it up with cooked veggies like carrot, cauliflower, and cubed squash and proteins like tofu, beans, or firm lentils.

1 acorn squash

1 yellow onion, chopped

2 garlic cloves, chopped

2 celery stalks, coarsely chopped

1 tablespoon water, plus more as needed

2 tablespoons whole wheat flour

2 cups no-sodium vegetable broth

1 teaspoon curry powder, plus more for seasoning

½ teaspoon dill

⅛ teaspoon cayenne pepper

1 (14-ounce) can full-fat coconut milk

Chopped scallions, green parts only, for serving

1. Preheat the oven to 350°F.

2. Halve the acorn squash lengthwise and scoop out the seeds and stringy center. Place the squash halves, cut-side down, in a 9-by-13-inch baking dish and add enough water to come up about 1 inch all around.

3. Bake for 30 to 45 minutes, or until the squash is easily pierced with a fork. Remove the squash from the baking dish and let cool to the touch, about 10 minutes. Scoop out the soft flesh and set aside in a bowl.

4. In an 8-quart pot over high heat, combine the onion, garlic, and celery. Sauté for 2 to 3 minutes, adding water, 1 tablespoon at a time, to prevent burning, until the onion is translucent but not browned.

5. Sprinkle in the flour and stir to coat the vegetables.

6. Add the vegetable broth, roasted squash, curry powder, dill, and cayenne pepper. Bring the mixture to a boil. Reduce the heat to maintain a simmer, cover the pot, and cook for 10 minutes.

7. Pour in the coconut milk. Using an immersion blender, blend the soup until smooth. Serve immediately or refrigerate in an airtight container for up to 1 week.

8. Top with scallions and a sprinkle of curry powder.

Tip: This soup benefits from the creamy coconut flavor of full-fat coconut milk. The mouthfeel is also enhanced by the natural oils in coconut.

Per Serving Calories: 169; Fat: 13g; Protein: 2g; Carbohydrates: 14g; Fiber: 2g

CREAMY TOMATO SOUP

Prep time: 10 minutes ⋆ **Cook time:** 35 minutes ⋆ **Serves:** 4

GLUTEN-FREE ONE POT

Tomato soup can be earthy and warming, or it can be overly sweet and citrusy. The process is what determines the outcome. When making tomato soup from scratch, the goal is to create a balance between the natural acid and sugar in tomatoes while creating a rich tomato flavor that doesn't taste like marinara.

2 carrots, coarsely
   chopped

½ cup water, plus
   1 tablespoon and more
   as needed

1 yellow onion,
   coarsely chopped

2 to 4 garlic cloves,
   coarsely chopped

1 (6-ounce) can
   tomato paste

1 tablespoon
   Hungarian paprika

1 (28-ounce) can diced
   tomatoes

1 (14-ounce) can full-fat
   coconut milk

1 teaspoon dried thyme

No-sodium vegetable broth
   or water, for thinning
   (optional)

1. In an 8-quart pot over medium-high heat, combine the carrots and ½ cup of water. Cover the pot and cook for 10 minutes, or until the carrots can be easily pierced with a fork. Add more water, ¼ cup at a time, if the water evaporates while cooking. Drain and transfer the cooked carrots to a bowl. Set aside.

2. Place the same pot over medium-low heat and combine the onion and garlic. Sauté for 5 to 7 minutes, adding water, 1 tablespoon at a time, to prevent burning, until the onion is fully browned.

3. Turn the heat to medium-high. Add the tomato paste and paprika. Cook, stirring continuously, for 30 seconds to 1 minute.

4. Add the diced tomatoes, coconut milk, thyme, and cooked carrots. Bring the liquid to a simmer. Cover the pot and reduce the heat to medium-low. Cook for 10 minutes, stirring occasionally.

5. Using an immersion blender, blend the soup until smooth. Alternatively, transfer the soup to a standard blender, working in batches as needed, and blend until smooth.

6. Add vegetable broth or water to thin as needed.

Tip: You can make your tomato soup creamy by replacing the coconut milk with ½ of a peeled, chopped russet potato and boiling it with the carrots. The flavor and silky mouthfeel of the soup will change, but cutting out the coconut milk will dramatically reduce the calories.

Per Serving Calories: 292; Fat: 19g; Protein: 6g; Carbohydrates: 28g; Fiber: 7g

ROASTED EGGPLANT & LENTIL STEW

Prep time: 20 minutes ★ **Cook time:** 1 hour, 10 minutes ★ **Serves:** 8

Umami, one of the five basic tastes, can be described as savory. Typically, this taste is associated with meats, but there are plant-based methods of using foods' natural glutamate to enhance a meal. Processed foods contain monosodium glutamate to impart a big umami flavor and make customers crave the product more. This roasted eggplant and lentil stew uses a variety of plants and techniques to build a natural umami flavor that is rich and delicious.

1 large eggplant

4 carrots, coarsely chopped

4 cups no-sodium vegetable broth

1 cup dried brown or green lentils

1 large yellow onion, diced

1 bunch chopped scallions, white and green parts, divided

3 garlic cloves, diced

1 tablespoon water, plus more as needed

1 (14-ounce) can full-fat coconut milk

1 tablespoon red miso paste

1 tablespoon low-sodium soy sauce

1. Preheat the oven to 350°F.

2. Halve the eggplant lengthwise and place it on a baking sheet, flesh-side up. Spread the carrots around the eggplant on the same baking sheet.

3. Roast for 30 minutes, or until the eggplant and carrots are lightly browned or caramel colored and the carrots are fork-tender.

4. Set the carrots aside. Let the eggplant cool before handling it. Scoop out as much flesh as possible without scooping into the skin and set aside in a bowl.

5. In an 8-quart pot over high heat, bring the vegetable broth to a boil. Lower the heat to maintain a simmer and add the lentils. Cover the pot and cook for 20 to 30 minutes, or until the lentils are soft yet retain their shape.

1 (28-ounce) can
  diced tomatoes

4 teaspoons ground cumin

1 teaspoon adobo
  chili powder or
  smoked paprika

1 celery stalk,
  coarsely chopped

Fresh cilantro leaves,
  for serving

6. While the lentils cook, in a small sauté pan or skillet over medium heat, cook the onion, white parts of the scallion, and garlic for 7 to 10 minutes, adding water, 1 tablespoon at a time, to prevent burning, until darkly browned.

7. In a blender, combine the roasted eggplant and onion mixture with the coconut milk, miso paste, and soy sauce. Puree for 2 to 3 minutes until smooth.

8. Once the lentils are finished cooking, add the tomatoes, cumin, chili powder, and celery. Bring the mixture to a simmer. Pour in the eggplant sauce and add the roasted carrots. Cook until warmed to your liking.

9. This stew is best served with a few fresh cilantro leaves and scallion greens on top.

Tip: This stew can be prepped ahead by roasting the eggplant and carrots, then refrigerating them in an airtight container for a quicker meal creation.

Per Serving Calories: 259; Fat: 10g; Protein: 10g; Carbohydrates: 35g; Fiber: 9g

TEX-MEX QUINOA VEGETABLE SOUP

Prep time: 20 minutes ★ **Cook time:** 3 to 8 hours in a slow cooker, or 1 hour on the stovetop ★ **Serves:** 6

GLUTEN-FREE · NUT-FREE · ONE POT

The flavors of this soup come from the natural sweetness of corn, carrots, and tomatoes, balanced with beans and nutty-tasting quinoa. Serve this soup with a generous portion of chopped avocado, a squeeze of fresh lime juice, and a sprinkle of fresh cilantro.

1 cup dried quinoa

½ large yellow onion, diced

2 garlic cloves, minced

2 carrots, cut into coins

2 celery stalks, cut into slices

1 tablespoon water, plus more as needed

¼ cup tomato paste

1 zucchini, cut into coins and quartered

1 (14-ounce) can whole-kernel corn, drained

1 (14-ounce) can diced tomatoes

1 (15-ounce) black beans, drained and rinsed

1 (15-ounce) can red kidney beans, drained and rinsed

2 teaspoons chili powder

1. Place the quinoa in a fine-mesh sieve and rinse under cold water for 2 to 3 minutes, or until the cloudy water becomes clear.

2. On a 5-quart or larger slow cooker, set the temperature to High and let it heat for 5 to 10 minutes.

3. In the preheated slow cooker, combine the onion, garlic, carrots, celery, and 1 tablespoon of water. Cook for 2 to 3 minutes. Stir in the tomato paste to combine.

4. Add the zucchini, corn, tomatoes, black beans, kidney beans, chili powder, cumin, and vegetable broth. Stir well. The tomato paste will fully incorporate as the soup cooks.

5. Turn the heat to low. Cover the slow cooker and cook on Low for 6 to 8 hours or cook on High for 3 to 4 hours. If the soup seems too thick, add more broth or water, ½ cup at a time.

1 teaspoon ground cumin

6 cups no-sodium vegetable broth, plus more as needed

6. Refrigerate leftovers in an airtight container for up to 1 week or freeze for 4 to 6 months.

Tip: To cook this soup on the stovetop, follow steps 1 through 5, but in step 5, cook the soup over medium-low heat, covered, for 45 to 60 minutes. Stir occasionally to prevent the tomatoes from settling to the bottom and scorching.

Tip: Black beans and kidney beans are the most common types used for Tex-Mex–style meals, but use any variety you prefer. This recipe is also delicious with jalapeño peppers or other hot peppers.

Per Serving Calories: 334; Fat: 4g; Protein: 16g; Carbohydrates: 62g; Fiber: 14g

ASPARAGUS & LEEK SOUP

Prep time: 15 minutes ⋆ **Cook time:** 35 minutes ⋆ **Serves:** 4

GLUTEN-FREE NUT-FREE

This protein- and fiber-rich soup is a delicious use of seasonal vegetables. Asparagus is typically served as a side dish, but it deserves to be the star thanks to its unique savory flavor and nutritional benefits.

2 leeks

1 tablespoon water

2 garlic cloves, minced

¾ teaspoon dried tarragon
(or dried dill or thyme)

1 cup dried red lentils

1 pound asparagus, cut into
1-inch pieces, including
the ends

6 cups no-sodium
vegetable broth

Juice of 1 lemon

Fresh ground black pepper

1. Cut off the leeks' root ends and the dark green portion of the stalks. Slit the remaining white and light green portion lengthwise down the center and run the leeks under cool water, using your fingers to remove any dirt between the layers. Thinly slice the leeks.

2. In a large pot over medium-high heat, combine the leeks and water. Sauté for 5 minutes. Add the garlic and tarragon. Cook for 2 minutes more.

3. Add the lentils, asparagus, and vegetable broth. Bring the soup to a boil, cover the pot, reduce the heat to medium-low, and cook for 20 to 30 minutes until the lentils are tender.

4. Remove some of the cooked lentils, leeks, and asparagus if you'd like some larger pieces in your soup. Using an immersion blender, puree the soup until smooth, or slightly chunky if preferred. Stir in the ingredients removed, if using.

5. Serve with a light drizzle of fresh lemon juice and season with pepper.

Per Serving Calories: 243; Fat: 2g; Protein: 16g;
Carbohydrates: 45g; Fiber: 8g

MISO, LENTIL & KALE SOUP

Prep time: 15 minutes ⋆ **Cook time:** 35 minutes ⋆ **Serves:** 4

GLUTEN-FREE NUT-FREE ONE POT

Lentils are high in fiber, iron, protein, and a broad range of phytochemicals that protect against type 2 diabetes and heart disease. The most common lentil, the brown lentil, retains its shape during cooking and gives an earthy flavor to dishes. This recipe also uses miso, various root vegetables, and kale to create a nutritious dish full of umami.

2 garlic cloves, minced

2 small shallots, diced

4 large carrots, thinly sliced

4 celery stalks, thinly sliced

1 tablespoon water, plus more as needed

3 cups baby potatoes, halved and quartered

4 cups no-sodium vegetable broth

1 tablespoon red miso paste

¼ teaspoon freshly ground black pepper

3 thyme sprigs

1 cup dried brown lentils, rinsed

2 cups coarsely chopped kale

1. In a large pot over medium-high heat, combine the garlic, shallots, carrots, and celery. Cook for 1 to 2 minutes, adding water, 1 tablespoon at a time, to prevent burning, until the shallots and celery start to become translucent.

2. Add the potatoes and cook for 3 to 4 minutes.

3. Carefully pour in the vegetable broth. Add the miso paste, pepper, thyme, and lentils. Bring the soup to a simmer, cover the pot, and cook for 15 to 20 minutes, or until the lentils and potatoes are tender.

4. Add the kale and cook for 3 to 4 minutes until wilted.

5. Refrigerate leftovers in an airtight container for up to 1 week or freeze for 4 to 6 months. The lentils will absorb some of the liquid; add more liquid or enjoy a thicker soup.

Tip: The shallots can be replaced with 1 yellow onion, but shallots are less acidic and bring a slight sweetness.

Per Serving Calories: 292; Fat: 2g; Protein: 15g; Carbohydrates: 58g; Fiber: 12g

CHICKPEA VEGETABLE SOUP

Prep time: 15 minutes ★ **Cook time:** 30 minutes ★ **Serves:** 4

GLUTEN-FREE ONE POT

This simple soup is filled with colorful vegetables and a warming balance of turmeric, ginger, and garlic. Serve this as is or add whole wheat noodles, rice, or barley to make it heartier.

1 yellow onion, coarsely chopped

2 carrots, coarsely chopped

2 celery stalks, coarsely chopped

1 red bell pepper, coarsely chopped

3 garlic cloves, minced

1 tablespoon water, plus more as needed

2 teaspoons grated peeled fresh ginger

1 small cauliflower head, cut into small florets

1 teaspoon ground turmeric

1 teaspoon Hungarian sweet paprika

6 cups no-sodium vegetable broth

2 cups chopped kale

1 (15-ounce) can chickpeas, rinsed and drained

Freshly ground black pepper

Chopped scallions, green parts only, for garnish

1. In a large pot over medium-high heat, combine the onion, carrots, celery, bell pepper, and garlic. Cook, stirring occasionally, for 5 minutes, or until the onion is translucent but not browned. Add water, 1 tablespoon at a time, if it seems like the onion and garlic are cooking too quickly.

2. Add the ginger and cook, stirring, for 30 seconds.

3. Stir in the cauliflower, turmeric, and paprika to coat the cauliflower evenly with the spices.

4. Pour in the vegetable broth and bring the liquid to a simmer. Reduce the heat to medium-low, cover the pot, and cook for 10 minutes.

5. Add the kale and chickpeas and cook for 5 minutes to soften the kale leaves. Season with pepper and garnish with scallions.

6. Refrigerate leftovers in an airtight container for up to 1 week or freeze for up to 1 month.

Tip: Stop peeling carrots! Carrot skins are highly nutritious and contain high levels of vitamin C and beneficial phytonutrients. You can avoid peeling by washing and scrubbing your carrots well to remove dirt and debris.

Per Serving Calories: 173; Fat: 3g; Protein: 8g; Carbohydrates: 32g; Fiber: 9g

FENNEL & GINGER BUTTERNUT SQUASH SOUP

Prep time: 15 minutes ⋆ **Cook time:** 25 minutes ⋆ **Serves:** 4

GLUTEN-FREE NUT-FREE ONE POT

Ginger, garlic, and onion are considered the "tri-root" in several cultures, used often for their flavor and immune system support. This creamy soup is colorful, rich in a variety of vitamins and minerals, and can be prepped ahead for a quick meal option during a stressful week.

1 small yellow onion, diced

2 garlic cloves, minced

½ fennel bulb, cut into slices

1 tablespoon water, plus more as needed

2 tablespoons grated peeled fresh ginger

½ butternut squash, peeled and diced into ½-inch pieces

½ cauliflower head, cut into florets

4 to 6 cups no-sodium vegetable broth

¼ teaspoon freshly ground black pepper

1. In a large pot over medium-high heat, combine the onion, garlic, and fennel. Cook, stirring occasionally, for 5 minutes, or until the onion is translucent but not browned. Add water, 1 tablespoon at a time, if it seems like the onion and garlic are cooking too quickly.

2. Add the ginger and cook, stirring, for 30 seconds.

3. Add the butternut squash, cauliflower, and just enough vegetable broth to cover the vegetables. Bring the liquid to a simmer, cover the pot, reduce the heat to medium-low, and cook for 15 minutes, or until the butternut squash can be easily pierced with a fork.

4. Using an immersion blender, puree the soup until smooth. Add more broth if you desire a thinner consistency.

5. Season with pepper and serve.

Tip: Soups like this can be easily prepared ahead by chopping vegetables and freezing them in labeled bags.

Per Serving Calories: 91; Fat: 1g; Protein: 4g; Carbohydrates: 21g; Fiber: 6g

MASOOR DAL STEW

Prep time: 10 minutes ★ **Cook time:** 30 minutes ★ **Serves:** 8

GLUTEN-FREE NUT-FREE

Dal (or daal) is a traditional Indian lentil stew that can be made a variety of ways by changing the spice combination, vegetable add-ins, or even the type of lentil. No two recipes are alike because most are based on family recipes. Here, the earthy flavor of the lentils is enhanced with traditional spices like cumin, coriander, mustard seed, and ginger to create a deeply aromatic dish that is warming and nutritious.

2 cups dried red lentils
(masoor dal)

1 tablespoon yellow
curry powder

1 teaspoon whole
mustard seeds

1 teaspoon ground
coriander

1 teaspoon ground cumin

8 cups water, plus
3 tablespoons and more
as needed

1 large yellow onion,
finely diced

6 garlic cloves, minced

1 tablespoon minced
peeled fresh ginger

1 celery stalk,
finely chopped

2 green chiles, minced
(and seeded if you want
less heat)

1 (15-ounce) can diced
tomatoes

Fresh cilantro, for garnish

1. Place the lentils in a fine-mesh sieve. Sift through them to look for stones or other debris. Rinse under cold water for a few minutes.

2. In a small dish, combine the curry powder, mustard seeds, coriander, and cumin. Set aside.

3. In an 8-quart pot over high heat, combine the lentils and 8 cups of water. Bring to a boil. Turn the heat to medium-low, partially cover the pot, and cook for 20 minutes. The lentils should be very tender.

4. While the lentils cook, make the *tadka*, or tempered spices. In a skillet over medium heat, combine the onion, garlic, ginger, celery, and green chiles. Cook for 5 minutes, adding water, 1 tablespoon of at a time, to prevent burning. The onion should be deeply browned and soft.

5. Spread the mixture out in the pan so that there is a small well or opening in the center. Pour the spices into the well and add 2 tablespoons of water. Cook for 1 minute, stirring continuously, slowly mixing the spices into the cooked vegetables.

6. Carefully add the tomatoes and stir to combine. Cook over medium-low heat for 7 minutes, stirring frequently.

7. Add the *tadka* to the cooked lentils, stir well, and cook for 5 minutes over medium heat. Serve immediately, garnished with cilantro, or refrigerate and serve the following day. Dal gets more flavorful with a day or two of resting in the refrigerator.

Tip: Tempering the spices before mixing them into the stew is a common cooking technique in Indian cuisine. This process, called *tadka*, brings out aromas and flavors in spices that would typically be flatter. Whole mustard seeds are often used in Indian recipes, but for this recipe you can use 1½ teaspoons of ground mustard in place of the mustard seeds if you prefer.

Per Serving Calories: 206; Fat: 1g; Protein: 13g; Carbohydrates: 37g; Fiber: 7g

SWEET POTATO GNOCCHI • PAGE 118

- 6 -

MAINS

MAINS

continued

BAKED FALAFEL

Prep time: 15 minutes, plus overnight ★ **Cook time:** 30 minutes ★ **Serves:** 6

GLUTEN-FREE   NUT-FREE

Good news! You can enjoy oil-free falafel by baking it. Wrap it in a pita and top with diced tomato, cucumber, and Cashew Sour Cream (page 168).

1 cup dried chickpeas

½ cup packed chopped fresh parsley

½ cup packed chopped fresh cilantro (or parsley if preferred)

½ cup chopped yellow onion

3 garlic cloves, peeled

1½ tablespoons chickpea flour or wheat flour (if gluten is not a concern)

2 teaspoons ground cumin

1 teaspoon ground coriander

½ teaspoon baking powder

2 tablespoons freshly squeezed lemon juice

1. The night before making falafel, in a large bowl, combine the dried chickpeas with enough water to cover by 3 inches. Cover the bowl and soak for at least 8 hours or overnight. Drain.

2. Preheat the oven to 375°F. Line a baking sheet with parchment paper.

3. In a high-speed blender or food processor, combine the soaked chickpeas, parsley, cilantro, onion, garlic, flour, cumin, coriander, baking powder, and lemon juice. Pulse until all ingredients are well combined but not smooth; it should have the consistency of sand but stick together when pressed.

4. Using a cookie scoop or two spoons, divide the falafel mixture into 20 balls and place them on the prepared baking sheet. Lightly flatten each ball using the bottom of a measuring cup. This will help them cook more evenly.

5. Bake for 15 minutes. Flip. Bake for 10 to 15 minutes more, until lightly browned.

6. Refrigerate in an airtight container for up to 1 week or freeze for up to 1 month.

Per Serving Calories: 129; Fat: 2g; Protein: 7g; Carbohydrates: 22g; Fiber: 6g

LENTIL & VEGETABLE LOAF

Prep time: 45 minutes ★ **Cook time:** 1 hour, 40 minutes ★ **Serves:** 8

GLUTEN-FREE   NUT-FREE

This lentil loaf is a good starter recipe for those transitioning to the whole-food, plant-based diet because it covers oil-free sautéing, preparing lentils, and using seasoning without salt. To make this an iconic meal, serve with a side of roasted potatoes and sautéed garlic green beans.

For the glaze (optional)

- 3 tablespoons tomato paste
- 2 tablespoons pure maple syrup
- 1 tablespoon apple cider vinegar
- ¼ teaspoon garlic powder

For the lentil loaf

- 1 cup dried brown lentils, rinsed and picked over for stones and debris
- 2½ cups no-sodium vegetable broth
- Olive oil cooking spray, for coating
- 1 tablespoon nutritional yeast
- 1 teaspoon dried thyme
- 1 teaspoon onion powder
- 1 teaspoon paprika
- ½ teaspoon ground cumin
- ½ teaspoon garlic powder

To make the glaze (if using)

1. In a small bowl, whisk together the tomato paste, maple syrup, vinegar, and garlic powder until smooth. Set aside.

To make the lentil loaf

2. In a large pot over high heat, combine the lentils and vegetable broth. Bring to a boil, reduce the heat to medium-low, cover the pot, and simmer for 35 minutes, stirring occasionally. The lentils are done when they are soft and can be pureed. Set aside to cool without draining, at least 15 minutes.

3. Preheat the oven to 350°F. Create a parchment-paper sling for a 9-inch loaf pan by cutting a piece of parchment paper that can be inserted into the tin lengthwise with the sides slightly overhanging. Spray the inside of the pan lightly with oil and insert the parchment-paper sling.

4. In a small bowl, stir together the nutritional yeast, thyme, onion powder, paprika, cumin, garlic powder, and pepper. Set aside.

¼ teaspoon freshly ground
   black pepper

3 tablespoons ground
   flaxseed

¼ cup water, plus
   1 tablespoon and more
   as needed

3 garlic cloves, minced

1 small onion, diced

1 small red bell
   pepper, diced

1 carrot, grated

1 celery stalk, diced

¾ cup old-fashioned oats
   (not quick oats)

½ cup oat flour

5. In another small bowl, stir together the flaxseed and ¼ cup of water to make a flax egg.

6. In a sauté pan or skillet over medium-high heat, combine the garlic, onion, bell pepper, carrot, and celery. Sauté for 4 to 5 minutes, or until the onion is translucent. Add water, 1 tablespoon at a time, to prevent the onion from burning and sticking. Remove from the heat, evenly sprinkle on the spice mixture, and mix well to incorporate. Set aside to cool.

7. Drain any excess water from the cooled lentils and transfer three-quarters of the lentils to a food processor or a large bowl using a potato masher or heavy spoon, and puree. Set aside the remaining one-quarter of the lentils.

8. Transfer the pureed lentils to a large bowl and stir in the sautéed vegetables, oats, oat flour, and flax egg. Mix well.

9. Stir in the reserved whole lentils. Spoon the mixture into the loaf pan. Using a spoon or spatula, press the mixture into the pan.

10. If using the glaze, spread it evenly over the lentil loaf.

11. Bake on the center rack for about 50 minutes, or until the top is browned and crusted rather than wet. Let cool for 10 minutes before removing from the pan and cutting into slices.

Per Serving with Glaze Calories: 187; Fat: 3g; Protein: 9g; Carbohydrates: 33g; Fiber: 7g

CHICKPEA COCONUT CURRY

Prep time: 10 minutes ★ **Cook time:** 30 minutes ★ **Serves:** 4

GLUTEN-FREE

Making your own curry from scratch is a good way to learn about spice combinations and building flavor from the bottom of the pan up. This curry is quick and simple and, with just a few ingredients, you'll have a warming, flavorful curry to pour over your choice of rice, couscous, cauliflower rice, or serve simply in a bowl. The key to this recipe is to have your ingredients prepared, mise en place, by your stovetop for quick transitions between toasting your spices and pouring in the liquids.

2 teaspoons ground coriander

1 teaspoon ground cumin

½ teaspoon ground turmeric

¼ teaspoon freshly ground black pepper

¼ teaspoon cayenne pepper

1 large red onion, thinly sliced

3 tablespoons water, divided, plus more as needed

3 garlic cloves, minced

1 tablespoon grated peeled fresh ginger

1 (14-ounce) can diced tomatoes

1. In a small bowl, stir together the coriander, cumin, turmeric, black pepper, and cayenne pepper.

2. In a large pan over medium-high heat, combine the red onion and 1 tablespoon of water. Cook until the water evaporates and add another 1 tablespoon of water. Continue this process for 3 to 5 minutes, or until the onion is soft and just starting to brown.

3. Reduce the heat to medium-low and add the garlic and ginger. Cook for 2 to 3 minutes, adding water as needed to prevent burning, until the onion is browned. Evenly sprinkle the spice mixture onto the cooked vegetables. Cook, stirring slowly to toast the spices, for 30 seconds. Add 1 tablespoon of water and cook for 30 seconds more.

1 teaspoon garam masala

1 (14-ounce) can full-fat
coconut milk

1 (15-ounce) can chickpeas,
drained and rinsed

Juice of 1 lime

1 tablespoon chopped
fresh cilantro, plus more
for serving

Lime wedges, for serving

4. Carefully pour the tomatoes and their juices into the pan and stir. Cook over medium-low heat for 5 minutes, stirring. The tomatoes should be simmering and the pieces of tomato will start to soften and break down. Evenly sprinkle the garam masala on the cooked tomatoes and stir to combine.

5. Pour in the coconut milk and chickpeas. Bring the curry to a simmer and cook for 10 minutes, stirring occasionally.

6. Stir in the lime juice and 1 tablespoon of cilantro. Serve with lime wedges for squeezing and a few pinches of cilantro.

Tip: Mise en place, the French culinary phrase meaning, "putting in place," is a kitchen practice that can eliminate mishaps and the anxiety of having to rush while things are cooking. Measure all ingredients before mixing or cooking and have everything you need close by.

Per Serving Calories: 324; Fat: 21g; Protein: 8g; Carbohydrates: 30g; Fiber: 7g

SPICY SOBA NOODLES WITH SESAME PEANUT SAUCE

Prep time: 15 minutes ★ **Cook time:** 10 minutes ★ **Serves:** 4

GLUTEN-FREE QUICK

Soba noodles are made using buckwheat flour, which is naturally gluten-free and has a notable nutty flavor that pairs well with sesame, peanuts, peppers, and even mango. Buckwheat is an excellent source of fiber, and it is low on the glycemic index, meaning the carbohydrate energy provided is released slowly to prevent a spike in blood sugar. This noodle bowl can be customized based on what you have available in your refrigerator or what produce is in season.

For the peanut sauce

¼ cup smooth
   peanut butter

¼ cup warm water

¼ cup tamari

2 tablespoons pure
   maple syrup

1 tablespoon lime zest

Juice of 1 lime

2 garlic cloves, minced

1 tablespoon grated peeled
   fresh ginger

2 tablespoons red pepper
   sauce, like sriracha

To make the peanut sauce

1. In a small bowl, whisk together the peanut butter, warm water, tamari, maple syrup, lime zest and juice, garlic, ginger, and pepper sauce until smooth. The sauce can also be pureed in a blender for even easier preparation. Set aside.

For the noodle bowls

1 cup shelled edamame, thawed if frozen

1 carrot, shredded

1 shallot, thinly sliced

1 red bell pepper, cut into strips

1 small red cabbage head, chopped

1 bunch spring onions, chopped, divided

½ cup unsalted peanuts

1 (9.5-ounce) package soba noodles

1 tablespoon sesame seeds, toasted

Chopped fresh cilantro, for serving

To make the noodle bowls

2. In a large bowl, toss together the edamame, carrot, shallot, bell pepper, red cabbage, three-quarters of the spring onions, and peanuts.

3. Cook the soba noodles according to the package directions. Drain and rinse the noodles. Add the noodles to the mixed vegetables and pour on three-quarters of the peanut sauce. Using tongs or pasta spoons, mix to combine. Serve with a drizzle of the remaining sauce on top, a sprinkle of toasted sesame seeds, a pinch cilantro, and the remaining spring onions.

Tip: Sriracha is made with red jalapeño peppers, vinegar, and garlic. There are many organic brands offering sriracha made from limited natural ingredients. Avoid those that list sugar as the second ingredient.

Tip: If you don't have tamari, use the same amount of light soy sauce or ⅓ cup of coconut aminos.

Tip: This dish tastes great without oil, but if you'd prefer to use oil to boost the nutty flavor, add 2 tablespoons of sesame oil to the sauce.

Per Serving Calories: 624; Fat: 22g; Protein: 31g; Carbohydrates: 84g; Fiber: 9g

LENTIL SLOPPY JOES

Prep time: 10 minutes ★ **Cook time:** 35 minutes ★ **Serves:** 4

NUT-FREE

This childhood favorite is easy to prepare and made using all-natural ingredients. Combining the lentils with mushrooms and spices brings out an umami flavor that balances well with the naturally sweet and acidic tomato.

4 cups water, plus
   1 tablespoon and more as
   needed, divided

1 cup dried brown lentils

1 tablespoon paprika

1 teaspoon onion powder

1 teaspoon garlic powder

1 teaspoon dried parsley

8 ounces button
   mushrooms, chopped

1 onion, diced

1 red bell pepper, diced

1 carrot, diced

4 ounces tomato paste

1 tablespoon tamari

1 tablespoon pure
   maple syrup

1 teaspoon apple
   cider vinegar

Multigrain bread, pita,
   whole wheat buns, or
   romaine lettuce leaves,
   for serving

1. In an 8-quart pot over high heat, bring 3 cups of water to a boil. Reduce the heat to maintain a simmer and add the lentils. Cover the pot and cook for 20 minutes, or until tender. Transfer the cooked lentils to a bowl.

2. In small bowl, stir together the paprika, onion powder, garlic powder, and parsley. Set aside.

3. Heat a pot over medium-high heat. Add the mushrooms and cook for 3 minutes to remove their moisture. Add the onion, red bell pepper, and carrot. Cook for 3 minutes more, or until the onion becomes translucent. Add water, 1 table-spoon at a time, to prevent burning.

4. Stir in the tomato paste and cook for 30 seconds.

5. Stir in the tamari, maple syrup, and vinegar to combine. Stir in the spice mixture. Add the remaining 1 cup of water and stir to combine.

6. Stir in the cooked lentils, adding more water to thin, as desired. The mixture should be fairly thick. Serve on your choice of bread or wrapped in leafy greens.

Per Serving Calories: 236; Fat: 2g; Protein: 15g; Carbohydrates: 46g; Fiber: 11g

ROASTED RED PEPPER & FARRO BOWL

Prep time: 15 minutes ★ **Cook time:** 40 minutes ★ **Serves:** 4

NUT-FREE

Farro is a delicious grain high in fiber, protein, zinc, and some B vitamins.
Its name refers to a variety originating in ancient Mesopotamia.

1½ cups dried farro

4 cups water, plus
   1 tablespoon and more
   as needed

1 onion, diced

5 garlic cloves, minced

2 roasted red peppers

1 (15-ounce) can diced
   tomatoes

1 cup no-sodium
   vegetable broth

1 tablespoon tamari

1 tablespoon dried parsley

1 teaspoon paprika

½ teaspoon dried thyme

½ teaspoon
   cayenne pepper

1 (15-ounce) can red kidney
   beans, drained and rinsed

1. In an 8-quart pot over high heat, combine the farro and 4 cups of water. Bring to a boil. Reduce the heat to medium-low, cover the pot, and cook for 25 minutes. Add more water, ½ cup at a time, if the farro looks too dry.

2. While the farro cooks, in a sauté pan or skillet over medium-high heat, cook the onion and garlic for 5 minutes, adding water, 1 tablespoon at a time, to prevent burning. The onion should be browned but not burned.

3. Transfer to a blender and add the roasted red peppers, tomatoes with their juices, vegetable broth, tamari, parsley, paprika, thyme, and cayenne pepper. Puree until smooth.

4. Stir the sauce and kidney beans into the cooked farro. Cook over medium-low heat, stirring, until the sauce starts to bubble. Turn off the heat, cover the pot, and let sit for 10 minutes before serving.

Tip: You can either buy roasted red peppers or make your own for this recipe (see page 155).

Per Serving Calories: 412; Fat: 2g; Protein: 19g;
Carbohydrates: 85g; Fiber: 17g

ROASTED GOLDEN BEET CURRY

Prep time: 15 minutes ★ **Cook time:** 1 hour ★ **Serves:** 4

GLUTEN-FREE   NUT-FREE

Roasting golden beets with onions and garlic brings out their natural sweetness, which pairs well with coconut milk and curry powder. Serve this with green beans, blanched broccolini, and chickpeas for a hearty meal. You can make this recipe spicy or mild by adjusting the level of cayenne pepper.

1 large golden beet, peeled and chopped into 1-inch pieces (about 4 cups)

1 onion, coarsely chopped

3 garlic cloves, peeled and stemmed

4 cups no-sodium vegetable broth

1 (12-ounce) package silken tofu

1 tablespoon coconut aminos or tamari

1 tablespoon grated peeled fresh ginger, or 1 teaspoon ground ginger

2 teaspoons yellow curry powder

½ teaspoon ground turmeric

¼ teaspoon cayenne pepper

1 (14-ounce) can full-fat coconut milk

1. Preheat the oven to 400°F. Line a baking sheet with parchment paper.

2. On the prepared baking sheet, spread the beet pieces in an even layer and top with the onion pieces and garlic cloves.

3. Bake for 45 minutes, until lightly browned and fork-tender. Transfer to a large pot and place it over medium heat.

4. Add the vegetable broth, tofu, coconut aminos, ginger, curry powder, turmeric, and cayenne pepper to the pot. Bring to a simmer. Cover the pot and cook for 15 minutes.

5. Add the coconut milk. Using an immersion blender, puree until smooth. Or transfer the soup to a blender, working in batches as needed, and blend until smooth.

6. Serve with rice or a grain and add a variety of cooked root vegetables and greens, as desired.

Per Serving Calories: 259; Fat: 20g; Protein: 7g; Carbohydrates: 18g; Fiber: 3g

PESTO QUINOA-STUFFED PEPPERS

Prep time: 10 minutes ∗ **Cook time:** 30 minutes ∗ **Serves:** 4

DAIRY-FREE   GLUTEN-FREE

This recipe for stuffed peppers is a mix of fresh flavors that is easy to make ahead for a quick weekday meal or lunch option. Quinoa adds a pleasant crunchy texture and slight nuttiness that pairs well with the bold pesto flavor and natural sweetness of the red bell peppers.

4 red bell peppers, halved lengthwise and cored

1 cup no-sodium vegetable broth

1 (15-ounce) can no-salt-added diced tomatoes

¾ cup dried quinoa, rinsed

8 ounces fresh baby spinach

2 tablespoons Everyday Pesto (page 164)

1. Preheat the oven to broil. Line a baking sheet with parchment paper.

2. Place the bell pepper halves, skin-side up, on the prepared baking sheet.

3. Broil for 2 to 5 minutes, or until the pepper skins begin to blister and slightly blacken. Remove from the oven and preheat to 350°F.

4. In an 8-quart pot over high heat, combine the vegetable broth and tomatoes. Bring to a boil. Stir in the quinoa and spinach. Reduce the heat to medium-low, cover the pot, and cook for 10 minutes, stirring occasionally.

5. Fill the pepper halves with the quinoa mixture.

6. Bake for 10 minutes. Top the cooked peppers with the pesto and serve warm.

Tip: When using a broiler for peppers, it is important to check every minute to prevent burning. The goal is to soften the flesh and give the tough red pepper skin a little char, which adds flavor and texture.

Per Serving Calories: 257; Fat: 6g; Protein: 13g; Carbohydrates: 40g; Fiber: 9g

THAI-INSPIRED RICE BOWL

Prep time: 30 minutes ★ **Cook time:** 45 minutes ★ **Serves:** 4

GLUTEN-FREE

The creamy peanut butter and lime sauce for this recipe will become a favorite, and you'll want to pour it on everything. The sauce pulls together the nuttiness of the brown rice, the fresh edamame, and the brightness of the bell peppers. To make this an easier weeknight meal, prep a big batch of the rice and sauce ahead of time. You can use any leftovers in other dishes throughout the week.

For the peanut sauce

- 3 tablespoons creamy peanut butter
- 2 tablespoons freshly squeezed lime juice
- 1 tablespoon packed lime zest
- 1 tablespoon coconut aminos
- 1 tablespoon grated peeled fresh ginger
- 2 garlic cloves, minced
- ½ teaspoon red pepper flakes

To make the peanut sauce

1. In a medium bowl, whisk together the peanut butter, lime juice and zest, coconut aminos, ginger, garlic, and red pepper flakes to combine. Set aside.

For the rice bowl

1½ cups water

¾ cup brown rice

1 small red cabbage, shredded

1 red bell pepper, cut into slices

1 yellow bell pepper, cut into slices

1 cup shelled edamame

1 shallot, cut into slices

1 carrot, cut into matchsticks

¼ cup fresh cilantro, chopped

1 bunch chopped scallions, green parts only

Juice of 1 lime

To make the rice bowl

2. In a medium pot over high heat, bring the water to a boil. Stir in the brown rice. Bring to a simmer, reduce the heat to medium-low, cover the pot, and cook, undisturbed, for 35 to 40 minutes. Check the rice after 35 minutes to see if the water has been absorbed. Remove from the heat.

3. In a large bowl, toss together the brown rice, red cabbage, red and yellow bell peppers, edamame, shallot, carrot, cilantro, scallions, and lime juice. Serve with a drizzle of peanut sauce.

Per Serving Calories: 323; Fat: 9g; Protein: 14g; Carbohydrates: 54g; Fiber: 11g

ONE-POT SHAKSHUKA

Prep time: 10 minutes ★ **Cook time:** 20 minutes ★ **Serves:** 6

GLUTEN-FREE NUT-FREE ONE POT QUICK

Shakshuka is a filling tomato-based dish that can be enjoyed for any meal of the day! Traditionally a Tunisian breakfast dish topped with poached eggs and feta, this recipe is a highly flavorful dish that is sweet, savory, spicy, and salty using plant-based ingredients. You can plate it or set the pan on the table and eat family-style, scooping up sauce with pita. It can also be served over rice, couscous, or a hearty grain like sorghum.

1 yellow onion, diced

3 garlic cloves, finely chopped

1 green bell pepper, diced

1 jalapeño pepper, seeded and diced

1 tablespoon water, plus more as needed

2 bay leaves

2 to 3 tablespoons tomato paste

1½ tablespoons paprika

1 tablespoon ground cumin

1 teaspoon chili powder

1 teaspoon freshly ground black pepper

1 (28-ounce) can crushed tomatoes

2 tablespoons finely chopped fresh cilantro

1 (15-ounce) can chickpeas, drained and rinsed

¼ to ½ cup kalamata olives or green olives, coarsely chopped (optional)

1. In a large skillet over medium-high heat, sauté the onion, garlic, bell pepper, and jalapeño pepper for about 3 minutes, until soft but not browned. Add water, 1 tablespoon at a time, to prevent burning. Add the bay leaves and sauté for 30 seconds.

2. Add 2 tablespoons of tomato paste. Cook for 2 minutes, stirring constantly. If you want a thicker sauce, add 1 more tablespoon of tomato paste.

3. Stir in the paprika, cumin, chili powder, and pepper. Cook for 1 minute. Carefully pour in the tomatoes with their juices. Cover the skillet and turn the heat to low. Cook for 10 minutes, stirring occasionally.

4. Remove from the heat and discard the bay leaves. Stir in the cilantro, chickpeas, and olives (if using).

Tip: Adding more chickpeas or cannellini beans, tempeh, or soft tofu is a simple way to incorporate more protein to this dish.

Tip: This sauce is thick and has a tendency to splatter, so you'll benefit from using a lid and splatter guard in the final steps. Having all ingredients prepped also helps you avoid scorching the onions and garlic and splattering the thick sauce as it simmers.

Per Serving Calories: 136; Fat: 2g; Protein: 7g; Carbohydrates: 26g; Fiber: 7g

DECONSTRUCTED MALAI KOFTA

Prep time: 20 minutes ★ **Cook time:** 30 minutes ★ **Serves:** 4

Malai kofta is a North Indian specialty with a rich, spiced tomato gravy and koftas, a common vegetarian alternative to meatballs. Traditionally, koftas are made by mashing together paneer, a type of cheese, and cooked potatoes and then lightly frying before adding to the rich sauce. Here, the kofta ingredients are simply added to the sauce. Tadka, or tempering spices, elevates this recipe and is a crucial step for added flavor depth.

2 russet potatoes, diced

2 carrots, diced

1¼ cups water, plus 2 tablespoons and more as needed, divided

1 (15-ounce) package frozen sweet peas, or canned, drained

1 (28-ounce) can crushed tomatoes

1 (4-ounce) can diced green chiles

1 tablespoon minced peeled fresh ginger

3 garlic cloves, minced

1 tablespoon ground coriander

1 teaspoon ground cumin

1 teaspoon ground turmeric

¼ teaspoon onion powder

¼ to ½ teaspoon cayenne pepper

1. In a sauté pan or skillet over medium-high heat, combine the potatoes, carrots, and ¼ cup of water. Cover the pan and simmer for about 5 minutes, or until the carrots begin to soften. Top with the sweet peas. Remove from the heat and keep covered.

2. In a high-speed blender, combine the tomatoes with their juices, green chiles, ginger, and garlic. Puree into a thick sauce. Set aside.

3. In a small bowl, whisk together the coriander, cumin, turmeric, onion powder, cayenne pepper, and 2 tablespoons of water to combine.

4. In an 8-quart pot over medium heat, pour in the spice mixture and cook for 1 minute, stirring. Add more water, 2 tablespoons at a time, if the mixture looks dry. Tempering the spices by heating brings out a different flavor and is common in Indian recipes.

2 tablespoons tomato paste

¼ cup coconut cream

¼ teaspoon garam masala

¼ cup minced fresh cilantro

5. Stir the tomato paste into the tempered spices to combine. Cook for 2 minutes, adding more water as needed.

6. Pour in the pureed tomato sauce, stir well, and bring to a simmer. Reduce the heat and cook, partially covered, for 10 minutes.

7. Add the coconut cream, the remaining 1 cup of water, the garam masala, and cilantro. Mix to incorporate the coconut cream. Stir in the cooked potatoes, carrots, and peas. Bring to a simmer and serve warm as a rich stew or paired with basmati rice. Serve with chickpeas or baked tofu for added protein.

Tip: Traditional Indian recipes often include asafoetida (hing), a potent root reminiscent of onion, which could be used in this recipe in place of the onion powder. If using, add a scant ⅛ teaspoon, because a small amount adds a lot of flavor.

Per Serving Calories: 308; Fat: 5g; Protein: 13g; Carbohydrates: 59g; Fiber: 13g

SWEET POTATO GNOCCHI

Prep time: 50 minutes ∗ **Cook time:** 10 minutes (microwave); 1 hour (oven), plus 10 minutes for the gnocchi ∗ **Serves:** 2

5-INGREDIENT

Gnocchi is one of those recipes that people assume is too difficult, complex, or time-consuming to make at home. Is the potato riced or fluffy? Is it dry enough? Is it too dry? Sweet potatoes, with their high fiber content, make this dish a success on the first try. With just two simple ingredients, you can enjoy a foolproof gnocchi loaded with health benefits. It makes a delicious base for a variety of flavorful seasonings and sauces!

1 large sweet potato

¾ cup whole wheat flour, plus more for the work surface

4 quarts water, plus 1 tablespoon

3 garlic cloves, minced

2 handfuls fresh spinach

1 teaspoon crushed cashews

1. Using a fork or the tip of a knife, poke holes in the skin of the sweet potato. Microwave on high power, with the skin on, for 10 minutes, or bake at 350°F for 1 hour. The flesh of the sweet potato should be soft.

2. Halve the potato lengthwise and scoop the flesh into a bowl. Mash well using a fork. Add the flour and mix with a fork to combine.

3. Lightly dust a work surface and transfer the dough to it. Knead for 2 to 3 minutes. Roll the dough into a rope about ½ inch thick. Cut the rope into ¼-inch pieces. Lightly roll the tines of a fork across each piece to create grooves.

4. Bring 4 quarts of water to a boil over high heat. Reduce the heat to maintain a simmer and carefully place the gnocchi in the water. Cook for about 2 minutes, or until they float.

5. In a medium skillet over medium-high heat, heat 1 tablespoon water. Add the garlic and sauté for 1 minute. Add the spinach and cook, stirring, until it wilts. Add the cooked gnocchi and cook, stirring, for 1 minute more. Remove from the heat and sprinkle with cashews.

Tip: If you are eating this on its own, it will provide two satisfying servings. If you add a protein, like beans, tofu, or lentils, you can stretch it to feed more.

Tip: Gnocchi also tastes great with a drizzle of balsamic reduction (see page 59) or a simple dressing made with 2 tablespoons of freshly squeezed lemon juice, 1 teaspoon of grated peeled fresh ginger, and ½ teaspoon of ground cumin.

Per Serving Calories: 258; Fat: 2g; Protein: 9g; Carbohydrates: 55g; Fiber: 8g

ROASTED BEET BIRYANI

Prep time: 15 minutes ⋆ **Cook time:** 40 minutes ⋆ **Serves:** 4

GLUTEN-FREE   NUT-FREE

Biryani is a hearty rice main dish popular in Indian cuisine. There is no one specific recipe for biryani because the dish is made based on regional preferences of vegetables and spices. Typically, biryani is made by first mixing a curry of spices and vegetables and then adding cooked basmati rice. Basmati is a highly fragrant and distinctive rice that is low on the glycemic index, which makes it a perfect grain for the whole-food, plant-based diet. If you're able to find brown basmati, try it in a one-to-one ratio for the basmati.

6 cups water, plus 5 tablespoons and more as needed

2 cups basmati rice, rinsed well

1 teaspoon ground cardamom

½ teaspoon cayenne pepper

¼ teaspoon ground cinnamon

¼ teaspoon ground aniseed

¼ teaspoon ground turmeric

1 yellow onion, diced

3 garlic cloves, minced

1 (4-ounce) can diced green chiles

1 tablespoon grated peeled fresh ginger

1. Preheat the oven to 400°F.

2. In a large pot over high heat, bring 6 cups of water to a boil. Reduce the heat to medium-low, add the rice, and cook for 10 minutes. The rice will be parcooked. Using a fine-mesh sieve, strain the rice, lightly rinse, and set aside.

3. In a small bowl, stir together the cardamom, cayenne pepper, cinnamon, aniseed, and turmeric. Stir in 2 tablespoons of water. Set aside.

4. Heat a pot over medium heat. Add the onion, garlic, and 1 tablespoon water. Cook, stirring, for 5 minutes, adding more water, 1 tablespoon at a time, to prevent burning. The onion should be well browned.

5. Stir in the soaked spices and cook, stirring, for 1 minute. Add the green chiles and ginger. Cook for 30 seconds more.

1 large beet, peeled and finely chopped

3 carrots, diced

1 tablespoon yellow (mellow) miso paste

Oil, for coating

1 cup green peas

1 (15-ounce) can chickpeas, drained and rinsed

¼ cup packed chopped fresh cilantro, plus more for garnish

6. Add the beet, carrots, and 2 tablespoons of water. Sauté for 3 minutes, stirring. Stir in the miso paste and turn off the heat.

7. Lightly coat a 9-by-13-inch baking dish with oil. Spread half the cooked rice in the prepared dish. Top the rice with the beet and carrot mix, then the peas, and finally the chickpeas. Sprinkle the cilantro evenly across the top. Spread the remaining rice on top and cover the dish with aluminum foil.

8. Bake for 15 minutes. Lightly mix, garnish with cilantro, and serve.

Tip: You can also prepare this entirely on the stovetop. Follow the directions for baking but layer the biryani inside a pot and cook over low heat for 10 minutes, stirring occasionally. Let the rice sit in the pot, covered, for 15 minutes before serving. Traditionally biryani is made with ghee, a clarified butter. To mimic ghee's flavor, miso paste adds saltiness.

Per Serving Calories: 547; Fat: 3g; Protein: 18g; Carbohydrates: 112g; Fiber: 9g

THE BEST VEGGIE BURGERS

Prep time: 15 minutes ★ **Cook time:** 30 minutes ★ **Makes:** 12 patties

GLUTEN-FREE

Typically, lentil burgers fall apart with the first bite and they are more soft than chewy. The secret ingredient for this plant-based burger is uncooked sweet potato, which absorbs the moisture from the rice and lentils. This burger also gets a grain boost for nutrition and texture with coarse cornmeal. Using a couple of precooked ingredients speeds up the process.

1 yellow onion, coarsely chopped

3 garlic cloves, coarsely chopped

1 sweet potato, skin on, cubed

½ cup walnuts

1 cup precooked brown rice

2 cups precooked green lentils or brown lentils

1 tablespoon paprika

1 tablespoon tamari

2 tablespoons tomato paste

¼ cup water

1 tablespoon Dijon mustard or yellow mustard

¼ cup ground flaxseed

¾ to 1 cup coarse cornmeal

1. Preheat the oven to 450°F. Line a baking sheet with parchment paper.

2. In a food processor, combine the onion, garlic, sweet potato, and walnuts. Process for 1 to 2 minutes, or until the ingredients are combined and have the consistency of rice.

3. Add the brown rice, cooked lentils, paprika, and tamari. Pulse several times to incorporate the ingredients.

4. In a large bowl, stir together the tomato paste, water, mustard, and flaxseed. Add the blended ingredients to the bowl and mix to combine fully.

5. Starting with ¾ cup, stir in the cornmeal, adding more if the mixture looks too wet. The dough should form a ball without sticking to your hands too much. Divide the dough into 12 equal portions, roughly ¼ cup each. Roll the portions into balls and flatten onto the prepared baking sheet.

6. Bake for 15 minutes. Flip the patties and bake for 15 minutes more. The patties should be browned on the outside and firm to the touch. Serve immediately or let cool completely before freezing in an airtight container for up to 3 months.

Tip: Cooking the lentils and rice ahead saves time, and it allows them to dry out a little through refrigeration. However, you could make both the day of and spread them on a baking sheet to cool and wick off moisture while the oven preheats.

Per Serving (1 burger) Calories: 161; Fat: 5g; Protein: 6g; Carbohydrates: 24g; Fiber: 6g

HEARTY CHICKPEA BURGERS

Prep time: 15 minutes ★ **Cook time:** 10 minutes ★ **Serves:** 4

QUICK

These walnut and chickpea burgers will satisfy everyone with their rich umami flavors, juicy interior, and 11 grams of protein per patty. Serve this burger on a hearty wheat bun with slices of red onion, pickles, and any other toppings you can handle.

2 tablespoons ground flaxseed

¼ cup water

1 cup raw walnuts

½ cup whole wheat bread crumbs or gluten-free bread crumbs

1 garlic clove, peeled and stemmed

1 teaspoon chili powder

1 teaspoon smoked paprika

½ teaspoon garlic powder

¼ teaspoon onion powder

¾ cup canned chickpeas, drained and rinsed

3 tablespoons peanut butter

1 tablespoon apple cider vinegar

1. In a small bowl, whisk together the flaxseed and water. Set aside.

2. In a food processor, combine the walnuts, bread crumbs, garlic, chili powder, paprika, garlic powder, and onion powder. Process for about 2 minutes until crumbly. Add the soaked flaxseed, the chickpeas, peanut butter, and vinegar. Process for 1 to 2 minutes, or until fully combined.

3. Transfer the mixture to a large bowl and knead for 1 to 2 minutes, or until the mixture comes together and can be shaped. Divide the dough into 4 equal parts and shape into ½-inch-thick patties.

4. In a nonstick skillet over medium heat, cook the patties for 3 to 5 minutes per side until browned and crispy. Serve immediately.

Tip: These burgers should be cooked in a skillet before trying to grill them. Once cooked, they hold together well and can be transferred to a hot grill for a little char.

Per Serving Calories: 338; Fat: 25g; Protein: 11g; Carbohydrates: 22g; Fiber: 7g

CHEESY KIDNEY BEAN & BARLEY BOWL

Prep time: 20 minutes ★ **Cook time:** 50 minutes ★ **Serves:** 4

5-INGREDIENT · ONE POT

This recipe combines the heartiness of whole grains with a decadent cheesy sauce for a meal that will satisfy both kids and adults. Hulled barley takes more time to cook than the more common pearl barley, but it's used here because it is a whole grain and retains its shape and texture better once cooked.

1 cup hulled barley, rinsed

3 cups no-sodium vegetable broth

2 cups broccoli florets, chopped small

½ recipe (2 cups) Cheesy Vegetable Sauce (page 170)

1 (15-ounce) can red kidney beans, drained and rinsed

1. In an 8-quart pot over medium heat, combine the barley and vegetable broth. Bring to a simmer, cover the pot, and cook for 35 minutes, or until soft and chewy. Check the barley; if it still seems tough, cook for 5 minutes more before proceeding to the next step.

2. Stir the barley and vegetable broth. Place the broccoli on top of the barley but don't stir in. Cover the pot and cook over medium-low heat for 3 to 5 minutes. The broccoli should be tender but not overcooked.

3. Pour in the Cheesy Vegetable Sauce and red kidney beans. Using a spatula, gently fold to combine, rather than stir, to avoid breaking the broccoli.

4. Let sit, uncovered, for 5 minutes before serving.

Tip: If you can't find hulled barley, use another large grain, like farro or kamut, or a whole-grain pasta.

Per Serving Calories: 478; Fat: 12g; Protein: 23g; Carbohydrates: 74g; Fiber: 17g

ROASTED RAGU & WHOLE-GRAIN PASTA

Prep time: 15 minutes ★ **Cook time:** 45 minutes ★ **Serves:** 8

NUT-FREE

Roasting vegetables and tomatoes brings out a variety of complex flavors through the caramelization of the natural sugars, transforming a typically acidic sauce. This recipe requires little prep work or kitchen time, because most of the cooking time is combined while the vegetables roast. Serve this pasta with your choice of protein like tofu, tempeh, beans, or cooked lentils.

4 beefsteak
   tomatoes, halved

1 yellow onion, cut into
   slices and left as rings

2 large zucchini, cubed

2 large yellow
   squash, cubed

1 small red bell
   pepper, diced

3 garlic cloves, minced

1 teaspoon Italian
   seasoning

½ teaspoon freshly ground
   black pepper

1. Preheat the oven to 450°F. Line 2 baking sheets with parchment paper.

2. Place the tomato halves on 1 prepared baking sheet, cut-side up. Place the onion rings on the same baking sheet.

3. Roast on the center rack for 10 minutes.

4. While the tomatoes roast, in a large bowl, toss together the zucchini, squash, bell pepper, garlic, Italian seasoning, and pepper. Spread the vegetables on the other prepared baking sheet.

5. Place the vegetables on a lower rack (but not the lowest) and bake for 15 minutes. Flip the vegetables. Remove the tomato sheet and set aside. Move the vegetables to the center rack and roast for 15 minutes more.

1 pound whole wheat
  linguine

¼ cup tomato paste

1 teaspoon red
  pepper flakes

¼ teaspoon dried oregano

1 tablespoon packed
  minced fresh
  Italian parsley

2 tablespoons fresh basil
  chiffonade (see page 30),
  divided

6. Bring a large pot of water to a boil over high heat. Cook the pasta according to the package directions to al dente. Reserve ½ cup of the pasta water and drain the pasta. Keep the pasta in the strainer.

7. Return the pasta pot to medium heat. Transfer the roasted tomatoes and onions to the pot and stir in the tomato paste, reserved pasta water, red pepper flakes, and oregano. You can mash the tomatoes and onion using a heavy spoon for a chunky texture, or puree using an immersion blender, as you like.

8. Add the pasta, roasted vegetables, parsley, and 1 tablespoon of basil to the pot. Toss to combine and coat. Serve garnished with the remaining 1 tablespoon of basil.

Tip: To make this meal even faster, substitute 2 (15-ounce) cans of fire-roasted tomatoes for the beefsteak tomatoes. Canned tomatoes save time, but they often have a high sodium content.

Per Serving Calories: 272; Fat: 2g; Protein: 11g; Carbohydrates: 55g; Fiber: 5g

MUSHROOM RISOTTO

Prep time: 10 minutes ★ **Cook time:** 55 minutes ★ **Serves:** 4

GLUTEN-FREE NUT-FREE ONE POT

The key to good risotto is the rice. Arborio rice has enough starchiness to make a creamy sauce yet is hearty enough to remain chewy. The initial 20 minutes of undisturbed cooking time is also vital: Stirring too much will break down the rice structure, and you'll be left with a mushy paste.

1 yellow onion, chopped

3 garlic cloves, minced

½ celery stalk, minced

1 tablespoon water, plus more as needed

9 ounces baby portabella mushrooms, coarsely chopped

4 ounces shiitake mushrooms, coarsely chopped

1 tablespoon apple cider vinegar

1½ cups arborio rice

6 cups no-sodium vegetable broth, divided

1 (15-ounce) can red kidney beans, drained and rinsed

Scallions, green parts only, cut into chiffonade, for serving (see page 30)

1. In an 8-quart pot over high heat, combine the onion, garlic, and celery. Sauté for 2 to 3 minutes, adding water 1 tablespoon at a time to prevent burning. Add the baby portabella and shiitake mushrooms and sauté for 3 to 4 minutes, stirring, until the liquid from the mushrooms evaporates.

2. Sprinkle the vinegar over the vegetables, stir, and cook for 1 minute. Stir in the rice and sauté for 1 minute more.

3. Add 3 cups of vegetable broth and bring to a simmer. Reduce the heat to low and cover the pot. Cook, undisturbed, for 20 minutes.

4. Add 1½ cups of vegetable broth, stir, cover the pot, and cook for 10 minutes more.

5. Add the remaining 1½ cups of vegetable broth. Cook, stirring continuously but lightly, for 5 to 10 minutes more, or until the liquid has been mostly absorbed.

6. Stir in the red kidney beans. Serve warm, topped with scallions.

Per Serving Calories: 382; Fat: 1g; Protein: 14g; Carbohydrates: 80g; Fiber: 7g

CARIBBEAN-INSPIRED QUINOA BOWL

Prep time: 15 minutes ★ **Cook time:** 30 minutes ★ **Serves:** 4

GLUTEN-FREE   NUT-FREE

This Caribbean-inspired quinoa bowl combines the sweetness of pineapple and mango with the nuttiness of quinoa and the rich, earthy flavors of black beans and kale. Quinoa gives this recipe both a serving of fiber and a complete protein that is enhanced with the calcium-rich kale. This bowl is vibrantly colorful–serve it to someone you're looking to impress.

2 cups no-sodium vegetable broth

1 cup dried tricolor quinoa, rinsed

½ cup diced pineapple (fresh or canned in juice, not syrup)

2 cups kale, finely chopped

1 (15-ounce) can black beans, drained and rinsed

½ cup Mango Salsa (page 158)

2 scallions, coarsely chopped

1. In an 8-quart pot over medium heat, bring the vegetable broth to a simmer. Stir in the quinoa. Reduce the heat to medium-low, cover the pot, and cook for 15 minutes.

2. Turn off the heat and fluff the quinoa using a fork or spoon while adding the pineapple.

3. Top the quinoa with the kale but don't stir it in. Cover the pot and let sit for 10 minutes.

4. Stir the kale into the quinoa and serve in bowls with the black beans, topped with the Mango Salsa and scallions.

Tip: Making the Mango Salsa ahead saves time and allows the salsa flavors to meld while refrigerated. Substitute spinach or collard greens for the kale.

Per Serving Calories: 308; Fat: 3g; Protein: 13g; Carbohydrates: 58g; Fiber: 12g

WILD RICE & VEGGIE-STUFFED SQUASH

Prep time: 20 minutes ★ **Cook time:** 1 hour, 30 minutes ★ **Serves:** 4

GLUTEN-FREE

Roasted winter squash is visually appealing as a dinner table showpiece and a great way to get fiber and a wealth of vitamins. Squash typically deters people because of the hassle of peeling it, but this recipe skips that step and uses the tough outer shell of acorn squash as a makeshift bowl. Using wild rice offers a chewy contrast to the soft squash and cooked vegetables.

2 acorn squash, halved lengthwise

7½ cups water, divided

½ cup wild rice

1 cup no-sodium vegetable broth

1 carrot, finely chopped

½ yellow onion, finely chopped

1 cup cauliflower florets, chopped small

½ cup broccoli florets, chopped small

1 teaspoon garlic powder

1 teaspoon dried rosemary

½ teaspoon ground sage

¼ teaspoon freshly ground black pepper

¼ cup blanched slivered almonds, plus more for garnish

Chopped fresh parsley, for garnish

1. Cut off the stem from the acorn squash halves and use a spoon to remove the seeds. Don't peel or remove the skin.

2. In a large pot over high heat, bring 6 cups of water to a boil. Carefully place the squash halves into the boiling water and cook for about 15 minutes, or until the squash's pulp can be pierced with a fork. Using tongs, remove the squash and set aside to cool while you prepare the rest of the ingredients.

3. While the squash cools, in an 8-quart pot over high heat, stir together the wild rice and the remaining 1½ cups of water. Bring to a boil, reduce the heat to medium-low, cover the pot, and cook for 20 minutes.

4. With a fork or spoon, cut halfway into the cooked squash and remove the pulp. This will be added to the filling mixture. Reserve the squash shells.

5. Preheat the oven to 350°F.

6. Place the same pot you boiled the squash in over medium heat and bring the vegetable broth to a simmer. Add the carrot, onion, cauliflower, broccoli, garlic powder, rosemary, sage, and pepper. Reduce the heat to medium-low, cover the pot, and cook for 10 minutes. Stir in the cooked wild rice, squash pulp, and almonds. Evenly fill the squash cavities with the stuffing mix and place the filled squash on a baking sheet.

7. Bake for 15 to 20 minutes, or until the squash can be easily pierced with a fork and the outer skin looks wrinkled and lightly browned. Serve garnished with almonds and fresh parsley.

Tip: You can use other squash for this recipe based on seasonal or local availability. Acorn squash works best because of its mild, sweet flavor, but delicata or sweet dumpling squash also work well.

Per Serving Calories: 234; Fat: 4g; Protein: 8g; Carbohydrates: 47g; Fiber: 8g

CURRIED MILLET PATTIES WITH RED PEPPER SAUCE

Prep time: 20 minutes ⋆ **Cook time:** 1 hour ⋆ **Serves:** 4

GLUTEN-FREE NUT-FREE

Millet is a naturally gluten-free grain that has a nutty, almost corn-like flavor. This recipe combines those flavors with the earthiness of curry powder and peas with a slight sweetness from shredded carrots. Serve this as a main dish or on a bed of fresh mixed greens. Though harissa tops these patties, get creative and serve with Cashew Sour Cream (page 168) mixed with garlic and cucumber for a cooler flavor, with a chutney, or without sauce.

2 tablespoons ground flaxseed

3¼ cups water, plus 1 tablespoon and more as needed

5 scallions, white and green parts, thinly sliced

1 large carrot, finely shredded

2 garlic cloves, minced

1 tablespoon grated peeled fresh ginger

1 tablespoon yellow curry powder

1 cup dried millet, rinsed in cold water and drained

½ cup frozen green peas

1 cup Mild Harissa Sauce (page 171) for serving

1. In a small bowl, stir together the flaxseed and ¼ cup of water. Set aside.

2. In a nonstick sauté pan or skillet over medium-high heat, combine the scallions, carrot, garlic, and ginger. Cook, stirring, for 3 minutes, adding water, 1 tablespoon at a time, to prevent burning. Stir in the curry powder and cook, stirring, for 1 minute more. Turn off the heat once the scallions are tender.

3. Add the millet and stir to combine, coating the millet with the curry powder. Add the remaining cups of water and bring to a boil. Reduce the heat to medium-low, cover the pan, and simmer for about 15 minutes, until the water is absorbed. Turn off the heat, fluff the millet mixture with a fork or spoon, and let sit, covered, for 5 minutes.

4. Transfer the millet mixture to a large bowl and stir in the frozen peas. Let sit for about 10 minutes until cool enough to handle. Fold in the soaked flaxseed and mix well.

5. Line a baking sheet with parchment paper.

6. Form the mixture into 12 tightly packed patties, about ½ inch thick and 3 inches in diameter.
It is important to press them together firmly so they don't break apart while cooking. Place the patties on the prepared baking sheet until all the millet mixture is used.

7. Heat a clean sauté pan or skillet over medium-high heat. Add the patties, 4 to 6 at a time (you don't want to crowd your pan), and cook for 4 minutes per side, or until lightly browned. Be gentle when flipping so they don't break apart. Repeat with the remaining patties. Serve topped with the Mild Harissa Sauce.

Tip: Using oil in your pan will get your millet patties crispier. Unlike when you are browning onions with the water sauté technique, you don't want to use water for cooking the patties, because it will break them apart.

Per Serving Calories: 262; Fat: 4g; Protein: 9g; Carbohydrates: 48g; Fiber: 9g

CREAMY MUSHROOM PIZZA

Prep time: 45 minutes * **Cook time:** 30 minutes * **Serves:** 8

This pizza dough combines cornmeal and whole wheat flour for a crisp, crunchy texture that can hold up to a variety of toppings. The crust's flavor is slightly nutty with a mild cornmeal taste, and the flavor complexity is enhanced if you refrigerate your dough overnight before rolling it out. I recommend topping your baked pizza with fresh, chopped spinach.

For the cornmeal crust

- ½ cup warm water (less than 100°F)
- 1¼ tablespoons instant yeast
- ¼ cup cornmeal
- 2¾ to 3¼ cups whole wheat flour, divided, plus more for the work surface
- 1 tablespoon melted coconut oil (optional, see tip)
- ½ teaspoon garlic powder
- ½ teaspoon onion powder

For the topping

- 1 cup Cashew Sour Cream (page 168)
- 1 tablespoon nutritional yeast
- 1 tablespoon yellow (mellow) miso paste
- ½ teaspoon garlic powder
- 4 ounces shiitake mushrooms, stemmed and thinly sliced

To make the cornmeal crust

1. In a large bowl, stir together the warm water, yeast, cornmeal, and 1 cup of flour. Set aside for 10 minutes.

2. Add the melted coconut oil, garlic powder, onion powder, and flour—start with 1 cup and add more, ¼ cup at a time, so the dough comes together without being too sticky.

3. Lightly dust a work surface with flour and turn the dough out onto it. Knead the dough for 5 minutes. Place the dough in a sealable bag or a lightly oiled bowl and cover it. Let rest for 15 minutes, or refrigerate overnight.

To make the topping

4. In a medium bowl, whisk together the Cashew Sour Cream, nutritional yeast, miso paste, and garlic powder to combine. Set aside.

5. In a large skillet over high heat, combine the shiitake and cremini mushrooms and sauté for 3 minutes untouched. Add the onion and garlic and gently flip the ingredients to combine. Cook for about 4 minutes more, adding water,

8 ounces cremini mushrooms, stemmed and thinly sliced

½ large yellow onion, cut into thin strips

4 garlic cloves, minced

1 tablespoon water, plus more as needed

½ teaspoon dried oregano

1 teaspoon dried parsley

1 tablespoon at a time, if the onion is browning too quickly. The mushrooms should have some blackening and the onions should be browned.

To assemble the pizza

6. Preheat the oven to 425°F. Line 2 baking sheets with parchment paper.

7. Divide the dough in half and form the halves into round balls. Avoid using flour on your work surface because it can make the dough not stick to itself. Roll out or pat and stretch each dough ball into a thin layer, approximately 16 inches in diameter. If the dough isn't stretching, let it rest for 5 minutes and try again.

8. Place the shaped crusts on the prepared baking sheets. Bake for 8 minutes.

9. Spread the cashew cream sauce over the precooked crusts. Divide the mushroom and onion mix between the pizzas. Sprinkle on the oregano and parsley. Bake for 15 minutes more, or until the crust is golden brown.

Tip: Avoid using active dry yeast, as it requires a proofing stage and is less reliable. If you don't need two pizzas, refrigerate one of the dough rounds, covered, for up to 2 days, or freeze for up to 2 weeks.

Tip: The coconut oil in the crust helps keep it moist. If you'd prefer to omit it altogether, swap in 1 tablespoon of unsweetened applesauce.

Per Serving Calories: 285; Fat: 10g; Protein: 11g; Carbohydrates: 42g; Fiber: 6g

SPIRALIZED VEGETABLE LO MEIN

Prep time: 20 minutes ★ **Cook time:** 10 minutes ★ **Serves:** 4

NUT-FREE QUICK

Lo mein is a traditional Chinese dish with egg noodles and an unmistakable sesame flavor. This recipe swaps in spiralized vegetable noodles and reduces the amount of oil being used to just one teaspoon (compared to the 3 tablespoons most recipes call for). It's a delicious way to fill up on fiber- and nutrient-rich vegetables. Edamame is our protein here, but you could also use marinated and baked tofu, pan-seared tempeh, or any bean.

2 tablespoons low-sodium soy sauce

1 teaspoon sesame oil (optional, see tip)

1 tablespoon grated peeled fresh ginger

2 teaspoons pure maple syrup

¼ teaspoon red pepper flakes

1 tablespoon tapioca starch

2 tablespoons cold water

½ cup snow peas, halved

½ red bell pepper, cut into thin strips

1 large carrot, spiralized and cut into 3-inch-long strips

1 tablespoon water

1. In a small bowl, whisk together the soy sauce, sesame oil, ginger, maple syrup, red pepper flakes, tapioca starch, and cold water to combine. Set aside.

2. In a large sauté pan or skillet over medium heat, combine the garlic, snow peas, bell pepper, carrot, and water. Cook, gently stirring, for 3 minutes.

3. Add the zucchini, spinach, and edamame. Cook for 3 minutes to wilt the spinach and lightly cook the zucchini.

4. Carefully pour the sauce into the pan and toss the vegetables to coat. Cook for 1 to 2 minutes while the sauce warms and thickens. Serve immediately, topped with toasted sesame seeds. This dish is also delicious with a drizzle of sriracha and sprinkle of cilantro, if desired.

4 zucchini, spiralized and
cut into 3-inch-long strips
3 cups fresh baby spinach,
coarsely chopped
1 cup shelled edamame
Toasted sesame seeds,
for topping

Tip: The key to this recipe is to have all of the ingredients prepared ahead of time so that you don't overcook the spiralized vegetables. If you are spiralizing your vegetables at home, use firm zucchini so there isn't too much of a soft, watery center. The best carrots to spiralize are the large juicing carrots that you can often buy individually in the produce section.

Tip: Sesame oil is used here to boost the nutty flavor of the sauce, but it could easily be omitted or swapped for a bit of tahini.

Per Serving Calories: 141; Fat: 4g; Protein: 10g; Carbohydrates: 21g; Fiber: 5g

LENTIL BOLOGNESE

Prep time: 15 minutes ★ **Cook time:** 35 minutes ★ **Serves:** 8

NUT-FREE

This protein- and fiber-rich meal requires minimal prep time. The sauce is simple and gets the majority of its flavor from the slightly sweet and nutty red lentils with an added umami boost from the seared mushrooms. You can serve the sauce thick for a hearty rotini bowl or thin it with vegetable broth or coconut cream for a long noodle marinara.

8 ounces cremini mushrooms, chopped

1 yellow onion, finely diced

1 large carrot, chopped small

6 garlic cloves, minced

1 cup water, plus 1 tablespoon and more as needed

¼ cup tomato paste

2 teaspoons dried basil

1 teaspoon dried oregano

¼ teaspoon red pepper flakes

1 (28-ounce) can crushed tomatoes

¾ cup dried red lentils, rinsed and picked over for debris

1 pound whole wheat noodles

1. In a large sauté pan or skillet over high heat, cook the mushrooms for 3 minutes to remove their moisture, stirring to prevent burning.

2. Add the onion, carrot, and garlic. Cook for 3 minutes, adding water, 1 tablespoon at a time, to prevent burning, or until the onion is translucent and starts to brown.

3. Stir in the tomato paste, basil, oregano, and red pepper flakes to mix evenly with the vegetables. Cook for 1 minute.

4. Pour in the tomatoes with their juices, lentils, and 1 cup of water. Stir to combine. Bring the sauce to a simmer, cover the pan, and reduce the heat to low. Cook for 15 minutes, stirring occasionally. The sauce is done when the lentils are tender.

5. While the Bolognese sauce cooks, bring a large pot of salted (optional) water to a boil. Add the noodles and cook according to the package directions until al dente. Reserve ¼ cup of cooking water and add that to the sauce. Drain the noodles.

6. You can mix the noodles and sauce together or serve the noodles topped with the Bolognese. Mixing them together and letting them rest for 5 minutes before serving gives you the best results because the noodles soak up some of the liquid.

Tip: Cover your pot of water to reduce the time it takes to bring it to a boil. Salting the water is optional but it does season the otherwise bland noodles. Adding the ¼ cup of pasta cooking water adds a minimal amount of salt to the sauce but it is crucial to getting a glossy finish to your pasta dish.

Per Serving Calories: 336; Fat: 2g; Protein: 15g; Carbohydrates: 67g; Fiber: 7g

ALMOND FLOUR CRANBERRY
THUMBPRINTS ★ PAGE 148

-7-

SNACKS & TREATS

MINT BROWNIE DATE BARS

Prep time: 10 minutes, plus 15 minutes to chill ★ **Serves:** 6

5-INGREDIENT GLUTEN-FREE NO COOK NUT-FREE QUICK

This recipe uses the natural caramel taste in dates combined with cacao powder for a brownie flavor and texture. They can be customized in so many ways—adding nuts, dried fruits, and protein-rich flours. Dates are high in fiber, which improves gut health, and are a good source of the antioxidant phenolic acid, known for its anti-inflammatory properties. Dates are low on the glycemic index and may help lower blood sugar levels, which makes them a great snack choice.

1 cup pitted Medjool dates

1 cup old-fashioned oats

2 tablespoons cacao powder

¼ teaspoon mint extract

¼ cup cacao nibs or vegan chocolate chips

1. Sort through the dates and ensure there are no pits.

2. In a food processor, combine the dates, oats, cacao powder, mint extract, and cacao nibs. Pulse a few times to combine, scrape down the sides, and process until a ball forms. Shape the dough into a rectangle roughly ½ inch thick and cut it into 6 bars.

3. Stack the bars with a sheet of parchment paper or wax paper between them to avoid sticking. Refrigerate in a sealable bag for up to 2 weeks, or freeze in an airtight container for 4 to 6 months.

Tip: It is important to check your dates for pits before processing, because just one pit can damage your food processor blade or could ruin a whole batch of bars.

Per Serving (1 bar) Calories: 200; Fat: 4g; Protein: 3g; Carbohydrates: 39g; Fiber: 7g;

CARROT CAKE BALLS

Prep time: 10 minutes ★ **Makes:** 30 balls

`GLUTEN-FREE` `NO COOK` `QUICK`

This delicious snack or dessert is the perfect combination of chewy and cakey with a hint of natural sweetness. The high fiber from the carrot, coconut, and oats helps satisfy midday cravings while keeping your blood sugar even.

2 cups unsweetened coconut flakes

1 carrot, coarsely chopped

2 cups old-fashioned oats

½ cup smooth natural peanut butter

½ cup pure maple syrup

¼ cup coarsely chopped pecans

1 teaspoon ground cinnamon

½ teaspoon vanilla extract

½ teaspoon ground ginger

1. In a sauté pan or skillet over medium-high heat, toast the coconut for 3 to 6 minutes, stirring or flipping occasionally, until lightly browned. Remove from the heat.

2. In a food processor, pulse the carrot until finely chopped but not pureed. Transfer the carrot to a bowl and set aside.

3. In the food processor (it is okay if there is a little carrot in the bowl from the previous step), combine the toasted coconut flakes and oats. Pulse until coarsely ground but not until the ingredients become a flour.

4. Return the carrots to the processor and add the peanut butter, maple syrup, pecans, cinnamon, vanilla, and ginger. Pulse until the dough starts to form a ball. Divide the dough into 30 portions. Using your clean hands, press and form each portion into a ball.

5. Refrigerate in a sealable bag or airtight container for up to 2 weeks.

Per Serving (2 balls) Calories: 203; Fat: 13g; Protein: 4g; Carbohydrates: 19g; Fiber: 4g

TAHINI GINGER COOKIES

Prep time: 15 minutes ★ **Cook time:** 10 minutes ★ **Makes:** 12 cookies

NUT-FREE QUICK

Mildly reminiscent of gingerbread cookies, these tahini-flavored cookies can be enjoyed year-round. Ginger's subtle heat pairs with tahini's nuttiness and is balanced by the spices. Using whole wheat flour makes these cookies a whole-food, plant-based treat, but the flavor of the wheat adds to the overall complexity of these bite-size morsels.

¼ cup tahini

2 tablespoons pure maple syrup

2 tablespoons date sugar

1½ tablespoons oat milk, or other nondairy milk

½ teaspoon vanilla extract

¾ cup whole wheat flour, or a 1:1 gluten-free blend, plus more as needed

1 teaspoon ground ginger

1 teaspoon baking powder

½ teaspoon ground cinnamon

¼ teaspoon baking soda

⅛ teaspoon ground cloves

⅛ teaspoon ground nutmeg

2 tablespoons finely chopped dried ginger pieces

1. Preheat the oven to 350°F. Line a baking sheet with parchment paper or a silicone mat.

2. In a small bowl, whisk together the tahini, maple syrup, date sugar, oat milk, and vanilla until smooth.

3. In a large bowl, whisk together the flour, ginger, baking powder, cinnamon, baking soda, cloves, and nutmeg until fully combined. Add the dried ginger.

4. Fold the wet ingredients into the dry ingredients, mixing until the dough seems smooth and isn't too sticky. You can add more flour, 1 tablespoon at a time, as needed, but do not overmix. Divide the dough into 12 equal portions. Roll each piece into a ball and press them on the prepared baking sheet to about 1 inch thick.

5. Bake on the middle rack for 8 to 10 minutes until the tops are lightly golden brown. Transfer for a wire rack to cool. They will firm up as they cool but will remain slightly soft.

6. Store in an airtight container at room temperature for up to 1 week, or freeze for up to 6 months.

Tip: When mixing dough for baked goods, it's important not to over-work the dough, because your end result will be tough if you do. Use a heavy spatula, rather than a stand mixer, to fold the wet ingredients into the dry. When baking treats without oil, this is vital, because oil is used as a gluten inhibitor.

Per Serving (1 cookie) Calories: 73; Fat: 3g; Protein: 2g; Carbohydrates: 10g; Fiber: 1g

CHICKPEA COOKIE DOUGH

Prep time: 20 minutes ★ **Serves:** 8

GLUTEN-FREE   NO COOK   QUICK

This is a snack you will feel good about eating and serving to your friends and family. Chickpeas might seem like an unlikely candidate for a sweet treat, but by blending these soft legumes with some simple ingredients you get a protein- and fiber-rich treat. This cookie dough pairs well with apple slices for a kid-friendly snack or a sweet-tooth craving.

1 (15-ounce) can chickpeas

½ cup smooth natural peanut butter

2 tablespoons pure maple syrup

1½ teaspoons vanilla extract

½ teaspoon ground cinnamon

2 tablespoons pecans

1. Pour the chickpeas into a bowl and fill the bowl with water. Gently rub the chickpeas between your hands until you feel the skins coming off. Add more water to the bowl and let the skins float to the surface. Using your hand, scoop out the skins. Drain some of the water and repeat this step once more to remove as many of the chickpea skins as possible. Drain to remove all the water. Set the chickpeas aside. Doing this gives the final product a smooth consistency.

2. In a food processor, combine the chickpeas, peanut butter, maple syrup, vanilla, and cinnamon. Process for 2 minutes. Scrape down the sides and process for 2 minutes more, or until the dough is smooth and the ingredients are evenly distributed.

3. Add the pecans and pulse to combine but not fully process.

4. Refrigerate in an airtight container for up to 1 week.

Per Serving (¼ cup) Calories: 170; Fat: 10g; Protein: 6g; Carbohydrates: 15g; Fiber: 3g

MANGO PLANTAIN NICE CREAM

Chill time: Overnight ★ **Serves:** 4

GLUTEN-FREE | NO COOK | NUT-FREE

If you haven't heard of "nice cream," you're in for a treat. This plant-based ice cream will satisfy your sweet tooth without the high sugar and fat content. Most recipes use frozen bananas, but replacing the banana with a ripe plantain makes a big difference in both texture and nutrition.

2 plantains, peeled, cut into slices, and frozen

1 cup frozen mango pieces

½ cup unsweetened nondairy milk, plus more as needed

2 pitted dates or 1 tablespoon pure maple syrup

1 teaspoon vanilla extract

Juice of 1 lime

1. In a high-speed blender or food processor, combine the frozen plantains, mango, milk, dates, vanilla, and lime juice. Blend for 30 seconds. Scrape down the sides and blend again until smooth, scraping down the sides again if the mixture doesn't look smooth. Add more milk, 1 tablespoon at a time, as needed.

2. Refrigerate leftovers in an airtight container for a smoothie-like consistency, or freeze for a firm ice cream texture. If frozen, thaw slightly before serving.

Tip: The best ripeness for this recipe is when the plantain skin is mostly black with a little yellow showing. The plantain should still be firm to the touch but have some give, like a ripe peach. To prepare ahead for this recipe, cut your plantains into ¼-inch-thick coins and freeze them on a parchment-paper-lined baking sheet, then transfer to a freezer bag.

Tip: A standard blender won't be powerful enough to blend a thick mixture like nice cream. You can get a thick, creamy texture using a food processor, but you may need more liquid than the ½ cup in the ingredients list.

Per Serving (1 cup) Calories: 208; Fat: 1g; Protein: 2g; Carbohydrates: 52g; Fiber: 3g

ALMOND FLOUR CRANBERRY THUMBPRINTS

Prep time: 20 minutes, plus overnight to chill ★ **Cook:** 25 minutes ★ **Makes:** 16 cookies

GLUTEN-FREE

If you're craving something sweet but also simple and nutritious, these cookies are a perfect match. Thumbprint cookies get their name from their distinctive center impression filled with jam or jelly. This recipe uses an easy homemade cranberry jam, but you can change it based on your preference.

For the chia cranberry jam

- 2 cups fresh or frozen cranberries
- ¼ cup water
- ¼ cup pure maple syrup, plus more as needed
- 1 teaspoon vanilla extract, plus more as needed
- 2 tablespoons chia seeds

For the cookies

- ¼ cup pure maple syrup
- ¼ cup avocado oil (optional, see tip)
- 2 teaspoons vanilla extract
- 2 cups almond flour
- ¼ cup slivered almonds, crushed or chopped

To make the chia cranberry jam

1. Make the jam before starting the cookies, because the jam needs some time to set. The jam is best refrigerated overnight. If you are using a premade jam, skip to step 4.

2. In a saucepan over medium heat, stir together the cranberries, water, maple syrup, and vanilla. Cook, stirring occasionally, for 6 to 8 minutes. Once the cranberries begin to burst and split open, turn off the heat and use the back of a heavy wooden spoon or potato masher to break the rest of the cranberries. If you want a smoother jam, transfer the mixture to a blender and blend until smooth, or use an immersion blender in the pot. Taste and adjust the maple syrup or vanilla, as you like.

3. Stir in the chia seeds and transfer the jam to a glass jar or dish, cover, and refrigerate for a few hours, or overnight. The jam will thicken as it cools as the chia seeds soak up liquid and expand.

To make the cookies

4. Preheat the oven to 350°F. Line a baking sheet with parchment paper or a silicone mat.

5. In a medium bowl, whisk together the maple syrup, oil, and vanilla to blend. Add the almond flour and mix until a soft dough forms.

6. Place the almonds in a shallow dish.

7. Divide the dough into 16 equal pieces. Shape the dough by rolling each piece into a small ball. Roll each ball in the almonds, then press them down on the prepared baking sheet. Each cookie should be roughly ½ inch thick.

8. Use the back of a tablespoon-size measuring spoon, or go classic and use your thumb, to make an indentation in each pressed cookie. Don't press all the way through.

9. Fill each indentation with the chia cranberry jam so it just lines up with the top of the cookie.

10. Bake for 12 to 15 minutes. The cookies should be just turning golden brown.

11. Store the cookies in a covered dish at room temperature for up to 3 days, or refrigerate for up to 2 weeks.

Tip: The jam recipe makes enough for several batches of cookies, or you can refrigerate leftovers in a glass jar for up to 1 month or freeze for up to 6 months.

Tip: Avocado oil is used here to keep the cookies moist. If you'd prefer to omit it, swap in an equal amount of unsweetened applesauce.

Per Serving (1 cookie) Calories: 161; Fat: 12g; Protein: 4g; Carbohydrates: 12g; Fiber: 3g

LEMON-OATMEAL CACAO COOKIES

Prep time: 30 minutes ★ **Cook time:** 35 minutes ★ **Makes:** 14 cookies

GLUTEN-FREE

These cookies are chewy, chocolaty, and lemony. The pitted dates provide a rich caramel flavor, add fiber, and give the cookies a distinct chewy texture. The walnuts add heart-healthy vitamins and minerals and a slight crunch. The true star here is the combination of lemon and chocolate, which works well with the nuttiness of the oats and walnuts. Despite the prep time, these cookies come together with little work (the majority of time is soaking the dates).

12 pitted Medjool dates

Boiling water, for soaking the dates

1 cup unsweetened applesauce

1 tablespoon freshly squeezed lemon juice

1 teaspoon vanilla extract

1 tablespoon water, plus more as needed (optional)

1½ cups old-fashioned oats

1 cup oat flour (see tip)

¾ cup coarsely chopped walnuts

2 tablespoons lemon zest

1 tablespoon cacao powder

½ teaspoon baking soda

1. In a small bowl, combine the dates with enough boiling water to cover. Let sit for 15 to 20 minutes to soften.

2. While the dates soak, preheat the oven to 300°F. Line 2 baking sheets with parchment paper or silicone mats.

3. Drain the excess liquid from the dates and put them in a blender, along with the applesauce, lemon juice, and vanilla. Puree until a thick paste forms. Add water, 1 tablespoon at a time, if the mixture isn't getting smooth.

4. In a large bowl, stir together the oats, oat flour, walnuts, lemon zest, cacao powder, and baking soda. Pour in the date mixture and stir to combine. One at a time, scoop ¼-cup portions of dough, gently roll into a ball, and press down lightly on the prepared baking sheets. The cookie should be about 1 inch thick and roughly 3 inches in diameter.

5. Bake for 30 to 35 minutes, or until the tops of the cookies look crispy and dry. Transfer to a wire rack to cool.

6. Store in an airtight container at room temperature for up to 1 week.

Tip: You can make your own oat flour easily at home using a food processor. For 1 cup of oat flour, put 1½ cups of raw old-fashioned or rolled oats into a food processor and process for 3 to 5 minutes. Make it ahead and store it like other flours.

Per Serving (1 cookie) Calories: 174; Fat: 6g; Protein: 4g; Carbohydrates: 30g; Fiber: 4g;

PEANUT BUTTER GRANOLA BARS

Prep time: 10 minutes, plus 20 minutes to chill ★ **Makes:** 12 bars

GLUTEN-FREE NO COOK QUICK

Most processed granola bars have high sugar, fat, and sodium contents and include many chemicals for shelf stability. Making your own granola bars ensures fresh, quality ingredients and allows you to customize them.

1 cup packed pitted dates

¼ cup pure maple syrup

¼ cup creamy natural peanut butter or almond butter

1 cup coarsely chopped roasted unsalted almonds

1½ cups old-fashioned oats

1. In a food processor, combine the dates, maple syrup, and peanut butter. Process for 1 to 2 minutes, or until the mixture starts to come together and feels slightly sticky. Stop right before or as it starts to turn into a ball of loose dough.

2. Add the almonds and oats and process for 1 minute. Press the dough into an 8-by-8-inch baking dish and cover with plastic wrap. Refrigerate for 20 minutes.

3. Remove the dough and cut into 12 pieces. Refrigerate in a sealable bag or airtight container for 1 to 2 weeks, or freeze for up to 6 months.

Tip: If adding more nuts, seeds, or dried fruit, keep the total addition to under 1 cup so the bars retain their shape once cut. Transfer the dough mixture to a bowl and use a heavy wooden spoon to incorporate your add-ins. If adding seeds, I suggest sunflower, hemp, or pumpkin; stir them in last and use up to ¼ cup total. Toast your oats in a 350°F oven for 10 minutes to add even more flavor.

Per Serving (1 bar) Calories: 181; Fat: 9g; Protein: 5g; Carbohydrates: 24g; Fiber: 4g

CHICKPEA GUACAMOLE

Prep time: 15 minutes, plus 1 hour to chill ★ **Serves:** 4

GLUTEN-FREE   NO COOK   NUT-FREE

The price of avocados is often a deterrent to making fresh guacamole, but by bulking up your dip with a legume, you get both added volume and bonus nutrients. The added protein and fiber from the chickpeas also make this creamy dip more satisfying and lower the amount of fat per serving.

1 (15-ounce) can chickpeas

2 large ripe avocados, halved and pitted

3 garlic cloves, minced

½ small red onion, diced

½ small red bell pepper, diced

¼ cup packed chopped fresh cilantro

Juice of 1 lime

½ teaspoon ground cumin

1 jalapeño pepper, seeded and minced (optional)

1. Drain, rinse, and peel the chickpeas using the method described in step 1 for Chickpea Cookie Dough (see page 146). You can leave the skins on for added fiber, but your guacamole will be smoother if you remove the skins. Transfer to a large bowl. Using a potato masher, crush the chickpeas.

2. Scoop the avocado flesh into the bowl of chickpeas and mash to your preferred texture.

3. Using a spatula or spoon, stir in the garlic, red onion, bell pepper, cilantro, lime juice, cumin, and jalapeño pepper (if using). Scoop the guacamole into a sealable container and refrigerate for at least 1 hour to let the flavors combine.

4. Refrigerate leftovers in an airtight container. It is best if eaten within 2 to 3 days but will keep for up 1 week.

Tip: Avocados start to brown once the soft inner flesh is exposed to oxygen. To avoid this, press a sheet of plastic wrap directly onto the guacamole surface, then cover with your container's lid.

Per Serving Calories: 266; Fat: 17g; Protein: 7g; Carbohydrates: 27g; Fiber: 12g

CREAMY ROASTED RED PEPPER HUMMUS

Prep time: 20 minutes ★ **Serves:** 8

GLUTEN-FREE · NO COOK · NUT-FREE · QUICK

There are plenty of recipes promising "the best" hummus ever but, generally, the only difference is the addition or substitution of an ingredient. The best hummus is less about the flavor and more about the texture. The trick to fluffy, creamy hummus is quite simple—add the chickpeas last and remove most of their skins. This recipe skips the oil and uses roasted red pepper for added flavor. Don't like roasted red pepper? Skip it.

1 (15-ounce) can chickpeas, 3 tablespoons aquafaba (chickpea liquid from the can) reserved, remaining liquid drained, rinsed

¼ cup tahini

1 tablespoon freshly squeezed lemon juice

1 teaspoon Hungarian paprika

½ teaspoon ground cumin

¼ teaspoon freshly ground black pepper

2 garlic cloves, peeled and stemmed

2 roasted red peppers (see tip)

1. Pour the chickpeas into a bowl and fill the bowl with water. Gently rub the chickpeas between your hands until you feel the skins coming off. Add more water to the bowl and let the skins float to the surface. Using your hand, scoop out the skins. Drain some of the water and repeat this step once more to remove as many of the chickpea skins as possible. Drain to remove all the water. Set the chickpeas aside.

2. In a food processor or high-speed blender, combine the reserved aquafaba, tahini, and lemon juice. Process for 2 minutes.

3. Add the paprika, cumin, black pepper, garlic, and red peppers. Puree until the red peppers are incorporated.

4. Add the chickpeas and blend for 2 to 3 minutes, or until the hummus is smooth.

5. Refrigerate leftovers in an airtight container for up to 1 week.

Tip: You can roast red peppers at home by charring the skin on your gas burner or under your broiler until evenly blackened, then wiping off the char using a paper towel or under running water. However, to save time and avoid setting off your smoke detectors, buy roasted red peppers in brine at your grocery store.

Per Serving Calories: 99; Fat: 5g; Protein: 4g; Carbohydrates: 11g; Fiber: 3g

WHITE BEAN & SPINACH ARTICHOKE DIP

Prep time: 10 minutes ★ **Cook time:** 15 minutes ★ **Serves:** 8

`NUT-FREE` `QUICK`

This recipe blends cannellini beans with oat milk for a creamy base and gets its cheesy flavor from yellow miso and nutritional yeast. Pumpkin may seem like an odd addition but it adds fiber and color.

½ yellow onion, peeled and sliced

3 garlic cloves, coarsely chopped

1 tablespoon water

1 (15-ounce) can cannellini beans, drained and rinsed

½ cup nutritional yeast

2 tablespoons yellow (mellow) miso paste

1 tablespoon tapioca starch

1 cup unsweetened oat milk

1 (15-ounce) can pumpkin (see tip)

1 (1-pound) package chopped frozen spinach

1 (14-ounce) can quartered artichoke hearts, drained

1. In a medium nonstick sauté pan or skillet over high heat, combine the onion, garlic, and water. Cook for 3 minutes, or until the onion is translucent and just beginning to brown. Transfer to a blender and add the cannellini beans, nutritional yeast, miso paste, tapioca starch, oat milk, and pumpkin. Puree until smooth. Set aside.

2. Return the pan to medium heat and add the spinach. Cook for 4 to 7 minutes, stirring, to thaw the spinach.

3. Stir in the puree mixture. Cook for 3 to 5 minutes, stirring occasionally, until the dip begins to bubble and thicken. Add the artichoke hearts and stir to combine. Serve warm.

4. You can also put the pan, if it's heat-safe, under the broiler for 1 to 2 minutes to give the top layer a little crust and char.

Tip: Use the pulp from an acorn squash instead of the pumpkin for a milder squash flavor. See page 84 for information on preparing an acorn squash.

Per Serving Calories: 147; Fat: 2g; Protein: 12g; Carbohydrates: 23g; Fiber: 9g

REFRIED LENTIL DIP

Prep time: 25 minutes ★ **Cook time:** 25 minutes ★ **Serves:** 4

GLUTEN-FREE

The refried bean texture comes from the food processor or blender because lentils are challenging to mash. Cashew Sour Cream (page 168) adds flavor, nutrients, and creaminess.

2 cups water

½ cup dried brown or green lentils, rinsed

1 jalapeño pepper, stemmed

½ cup Cashew Sour Cream

1 (4-ounce) can diced green chiles

1 teaspoon onion powder

½ teaspoon garlic powder

1. Preheat the broiler.

2. In an 8-quart pot over high heat, bring the water to a boil. Add the lentils, reduce the heat to maintain a simmer, cover the pot, and cook for 15 to 20 minutes. The lentils should be soft and squishable. Drain and set aside.

3. While the lentils cook, wrap the jalapeño pepper in aluminum foil to prevent it from burning. Place it under the broiler for 5 minutes. Turn the jalapeño pepper and cook for 2 minutes more. Remove and set aside.

4. In a high-speed blender or food processor, combine the cooked lentils, roasted jalapeño pepper, Cashew Sour Cream, green chiles, onion powder, and garlic powder. Puree until the dip achieves desired smoothness.

5. Serve warm or cold with chips, pita, spread on a wrap, or as a dip for crudités, as desired.

Tip: You can omit roasting the jalapeño pepper, but this step cuts down on the brightness of the pepper and adds more flavor to the dip.

Per Serving Calories: 177; Fat: 7g; Protein: 9g; Carbohydrates: 21g; Fiber: 5g

MANGO SALSA

Prep time: 20 minutes, plus 1 hour to chill (optional) ★ **Serves:** 4

`GLUTEN-FREE` `NUT-FREE` `NO COOK` `QUICK`

This mango salsa is a sweet and bright way to enhance a smoky barbecue sandwich or top a crispy corn chip. The flavors are a balance of sweet and citrus along with the sharp bite of red onion. Mango has a mild fruit flavor that pairs well with traditional salsa ingredients, but substitute fresh or canned pineapple if you prefer.

2 ripe mangos, seeded,
  flesh chopped

½ red onion, diced

½ red bell pepper, diced

1 jalapeño pepper, minced

Juice of 1 lime

1 tablespoon packed
  chopped fresh cilantro

1. In a large bowl, combine the mangos, red onion, bell pepper, jalapeño pepper, lime juice, and cilantro. Stir to combine, while lightly pressing on the mango pieces to break them up.

2. Serve immediately, or refrigerate in a covered bowl for at least 1 hour to allow the flavors to come together. Refrigerate leftovers in an airtight container for up to 1 week.

Tip: Mangos in the store are generally underripe, but they will ripen within a few days on your counter. A mango is ripe when you can press on the skin and there is a slight give, similar to a pear or peach. The mango will also have a stronger, fruitier scent once it's ripe.

Per Serving Calories: 114; Fat: 1g; Protein: 2g; Carbohydrates: 29g; Fiber: 3g

FRESH CORN SALSA

Prep time: 15 minutes, plus 1 hour to chill ★ **Serves:** 4

GLUTEN-FREE   NUT-FREE

This corn salsa uses fresh ingredients for both their vibrancy of flavor and color and the many vitamins and minerals they offer. This salsa is reminiscent of a fresh pico de gallo, but with corn instead of tomato to make it less watery and a little sweeter. Serve this salsa as an appetizer with chips or as a topping for a taco salad or use it to bulk up a burrito.

3 cups fresh corn kernels or 2 (15.25-ounce) cans whole-kernel corn, drained (see tip)

1 cup quartered grape tomatoes

1 green bell pepper, cored and diced

½ red onion, diced

½ cup packed chopped fresh cilantro

2 garlic cloves, minced

Juice of 1 or 2 limes

¼ teaspoon freshly ground black pepper

1. In a large bowl, stir together the corn, tomatoes, bell pepper, red onion, cilantro, garlic, lime juice (to taste), and pepper. Cover and refrigerate for at least 1 hour before serving.

2. Refrigerate leftovers in an airtight container for up to 1 week.

Tip: The best corn for this recipe is fresh and roasted, on the grill or under your broiler, with a little bit of char on the kernels. The roasting caramelizes the natural sugars in the corn and adds the visual appeal of blackened edges on the kernels.

Tip: This salsa is meant to be mild with a slight natural sweetness to enhance other dishes. If you like it spicy, add 1 jalapeño pepper, seeded and diced, or 1 (4-ounce) can of diced green chiles.

Per Serving Calories: 143; Fat: 2g; Protein: 5g; Carbohydrates: 34g; Fiber: 5g

BAKED VEGETABLE CHIPS

Prep time: 20 minutes ★ **Cook:** 35 minutes ★ **Serves:** 2

GLUTEN-FREE   NUT-FREE

This recipe isn't completely salt- and oil-free, but it's far healthier than the bagged and processed vegetable chips at the grocery store. Making your own chips is easy, and you can experiment with a variety of vegetables for unique flavors and crunch. To get the best crispness, a mandoline slicer is preferred. If you don't have a mandoline, you can still enjoy these baked vegetable chips and you'll get to work on your knife skills.

1 pound starchy root vegetables, such as russet potato, sweet potato, rutabaga, parsnip, red or golden beet, or taro

1 pound high-water vegetables, such as zucchini or summer squash

Kosher salt, for absorbing moisture

1 teaspoon garlic powder

1 teaspoon paprika

½ teaspoon onion powder

½ teaspoon freshly ground black pepper

1 teaspoon avocado oil or other oil (optional, see tip)

1. Preheat the oven to 300°F. Line 2 baking sheets with parchment paper. Set aside.

2. Scrub the root vegetables well to remove the dirt. Wash and dry the high-water vegetables.

3. Using a mandoline or sharp kitchen knife, cut all the vegetables into ⅛-inch-thick slices. The thinner you slice them, the crispier they will be.

4. Place the sliced high-water vegetables on a clean kitchen towel or paper towel. Sprinkle with a generous amount of kosher salt, which draws out moisture. If you skip this step, your high-water vegetables won't crisp and will remain soggy after baking. Let sit for 15 minutes. Use a paper towel to dab off excess moisture and salt.

5. In a small bowl, stir together the garlic powder, paprika, onion powder, and pepper.

6. Transfer all the vegetables to the prepared baking sheets and place them in a single layer. Brush with oil, if using. Evenly sprinkle the spice mix on the prepared vegetables.

7. Bake for 15 minutes. Switch the pans between the oven racks and bake for 20 minutes more, or until the vegetables are darker in color and crispy on the edges.

8. Using a spatula, transfer the chips to a wire rack to cool. The baked chips will crisp within a few minutes of cooling.

Tip: You can easily make any starchy root vegetable into a delicious chip, but it is helpful to start with a guaranteed winner like a russet potato.

Tip: You can omit the oil entirely from this recipe, but your chips will be more dried than crispy. If you do omit the oil, keep a very close eye on them in the oven.

Per Serving Calories: 250; Fat: 3g; Protein: 8g; Carbohydrates: 51g; Fiber: 6g

REFRIGERATOR PICKLES ★ PAGE 182

- 8 -

HOMEMADE STAPLES

EVERYDAY PESTO

Prep time: 5 minutes ★ **Cook time:** 5 minutes ★ **Makes:** 1 cup

GLUTEN-FREE

Pesto is so versatile, and this oil-free version gives any dish a healthy, flavorful boost. Use it on top of some roasted veggies and legume-based pasta, in Pesto Potato Salad (page 65), or in Pesto Quinoa-Stuffed Peppers (page 111).

4 cups packed fresh
   basil leaves

¼ cup raw cashews

2 tablespoons
   nutritional yeast

1 garlic clove

¼ teaspoon freshly ground
   black pepper

3 tablespoons boiling water,
   plus more as needed

1. In a food processor, blend the basil, cashews, nutritional yeast, garlic, pepper, and boiling water until smooth. Add more water to thin until you have a smooth, slightly thick mixture.

2. Refrigerate in a sealed jar for up to 1 month.

Per Serving (2 tablespoons) Calories: 35; Fat: 2g; Protein: 3g; Carbohydrates: 2g; Fiber: 1g

ALMOND-LEMON RICOTTA

Prep time: 5 minutes ★ **Makes:** 1 cup

GLUTEN-FREE   NO COOK   QUICK

Almond-lemon ricotta is perfect for topping pancakes, waffles, fresh berries, or as an additional topping for toast smeared with a nut butter or on a bowl of Carrot Cake Oatmeal (page 41). This recipe is simple and comes together in a few minutes with minimal prep.

2 cups blanched slivered almonds (not sliced)

¾ cup cold water

2 tablespoons freshly squeezed lemon juice

1 tablespoon lemon zest

1 tablespoon pure maple syrup

2 teaspoons nutritional yeast

½ teaspoon almond extract

1. In a food processor or high-speed blender, combine the almonds, water, lemon juice, lemon zest, maple syrup, nutritional yeast, and almond extract. Pulse to combine, scrape down the sides, and puree until mostly smooth.

2. Refrigerate in an airtight container for up to 2 weeks, or freeze for up to 6 months.

Tip: Unlike a nut butter, this recipe shouldn't be stored at room temperature because of the added water and lemon juice. It is important to pulse the mixture a couple of times before processing completely so the sides can be scraped down and all ingredients can be incorporated.

Per Serving (2 tablespoons) Calories: 166; Fat: 14g; Protein: 6g; Carbohydrates: 8g; Fiber: 4g

QUICK MOLE SAUCE

Prep time: 40 minutes ★ Cook time: 25 minutes ★ Makes: 4 cups

Mole is a traditional Mexican sauce that combines the bitterness of chocolate with the acidic smokiness of roasted or dried peppers and tomato to round it all out. It's not sweet or chocolaty, and it can be made mild or with some heat. Everyone who makes mole has their own secret recipe—some require several hours and a long list of ingredients. This simplified recipe will give you a start to understanding its complexity.

4 dried pasilla chiles

2 dried ancho chiles

Boiling water, for soaking the peppers

1 yellow onion, cut into slices

6 garlic cloves, coarsely chopped

1 tablespoon water, plus more as needed

2 tablespoons tomato paste

1 jalapeño pepper, seeded and chopped

2 ounces vegan dark chocolate

2 tablespoons whole wheat flour

2 tablespoons cocoa powder

2 tablespoons almond butter

2 teaspoons smoked paprika

1. Cut off the stem ends from the pasilla and ancho chiles and shake out the seeds. Cut the chiles in half, transfer to a medium bowl, and cover with the boiling water. Let soak for 20 minutes. Drain.

2. In a large nonstick sauté pan or skillet over medium-high heat, combine the onion and garlic. Cook for 5 to 7 minutes, adding water, 1 tablespoon at a time, to prevent burning. The onions should be dark brown but not burned. Stir in the tomato paste and cook for 2 minutes to caramelize. Transfer to a high-speed blender.

3. Add the soaked chiles, jalapeño pepper, chocolate, flour, cocoa powder, almond butter, paprika, cumin, cinnamon, oregano, and vegetable broth. Puree for about 3 minutes until smooth.

1 teaspoon ground cumin

1 teaspoon ground
cinnamon

½ teaspoon dried oregano

2½ cups no-sodium
vegetable broth

4. Return the sauté pan or skillet to medium-high heat. Pour in the sauce and cover the pan. Cook until the sauce begins to bubble. Reduce the heat to low and simmer, uncovered, for 5 minutes, stirring occasionally.

5. Serve immediately, refrigerate in an airtight container for up to 1 week, or freeze for up to 6 months.

Tip: The dried pasilla and ancho chiles are part of the overall flavor of this sauce. Add other fresh peppers such as more jalapeño or habanero peppers for more heat, or add 1 tablespoon of adobo sauce for added depth of flavor.

Per Serving (½ cup) Calories: 114; Fat: 7g; Protein: 4g; Carbohydrates: 13g; Fiber: 4g

CASHEW SOUR CREAM

Prep time: 20 minutes ★ **Makes:** 1 cup

`5-INGREDIENT` `GLUTEN-FREE` `NO COOK`

This nut-based vegan sour cream is tangy and smooth with just a hint of cheesiness, and it's great for sauce bases or as a topping. You can make this recipe in just a few minutes, but soak the raw cashews first.

1 cup raw cashews

½ cup water

1 tablespoon freshly squeezed lemon juice

¾ teaspoon apple cider vinegar

1 teaspoon nutritional yeast

1. Soak the cashews in water to cover overnight in your refrigerator or in boiling water to cover for 15 minutes. Soaking overnight means your cream will be thick and cold right away. Drain and transfer to a high-speed blender or food processor.

2. Add the water, lemon juice, vinegar, and nutritional yeast. Pulse to combine, scrape down the sides, and puree for 3 minutes, or until creamy and smooth. You may need to scrape down the sides again, depending on your equipment.

3. If you used boiling water to soak the cashews, the sauce may seem thin immediately after pureeing. It will thicken as it cools.

4. Refrigerate in a sealable container for up to 1 week.

Tip: Depending on how long you soaked your cashews, you may need to add more water to reach a creamy consistency. Add water, 1 tablespoon at a time, scraping the sides and processing thoroughly before adding more water.

Per Serving (2 tablespoons) Calories: 91; Fat: 7g; Protein: 3g; Carbohydrates: 5g; Fiber: 1g

CHICKENLESS BOUILLON BASE

Prep time: 5 minutes ★ **Makes:** 2 cups

GLUTEN-FREE   NO COOK   NUT-FREE   QUICK

Bouillon base is a simple way to add flavor to soups, stews, or sauces. The many commercial bouillon options often come with added MSG and a lot of sodium. By making your own, you control the ingredients. Because this recipe is made entirely with dried ingredients, the finished product is shelf-stable for several months. You can easily double or triple this recipe, and substitute herbs for unique flavor combinations.

2 cups nutritional yeast

¼ cup sea salt
  (optional, see tip)

2 tablespoons
  onion powder

1 tablespoon Italian
  seasoning

2 teaspoons garlic powder

1 teaspoon ground turmeric

1 teaspoon celery salt

1 teaspoon dried thyme

1. In a small blender, food processor, spice grinder, or mortar and pestle, combine the nutritional yeast, salt (if using), onion powder, Italian seasoning, garlic powder, turmeric, celery salt, and thyme. Blend to a powder.

2. Store the bouillon powder in a sealable jar or container at room temperature. Use 1 tablespoon per 1 cup of water for a flavorful stock.

Tip: If you omit the sea salt, I recommend adding more celery salt. Celery salt still contains salt, but it contains far less sodium, making it a WFPB-friendly alternative.

Tip: Just like any dried herb, the flavors lose potency with age and it's best to use this bouillon powder within 3 months. Store your herbs and spices away from direct sunlight to slow the aging process and avoid discoloration.

Per Serving (1 tablespoon) Calories: 23; Fat: 0g; Protein: 3g; Carbohydrates: 3g; Fiber: 1g

CHEESY VEGETABLE SAUCE

Prep time: 10 minutes ★ **Cook time:** 25 minutes ★ **Makes:** 4 cups

GLUTEN-FREE

Many dairy-free cheese sauce recipes rely on replacing dairy cheese with nondairy cheese and using oil instead of butter. This recipe uses whole-food, plant-based ingredients to make a smooth, cheesy sauce you can use for macaroni and cheese, tacos, queso dip, or even a broccoli cheese soup. Get creative by swapping in sunflower seeds and sweet potatoes and adding sun-dried tomatoes.

1 cup raw cashews

1 russet potato, peeled and cubed

2 carrots, cubed

½ cup nutritional yeast

2 tablespoons yellow (mellow) miso paste

1 teaspoon ground mustard

2 cups unsweetened oat milk (or almond or cashew if gluten-free)

1 tablespoon arrowroot powder, cornstarch, or tapioca starch

1 onion, chopped

3 garlic cloves, minced

1 tablespoon water, plus more as needed

1. In an 8-quart pot, combine the cashews, potato, and carrots. Add enough water to cover by 2 inches. Bring to a boil over high heat, then reduce the heat to simmer. Cook for 15 minutes.

2. In a blender, combine the nutritional yeast, miso paste, ground mustard, milk, and arrowroot powder.

3. Drain the cashews, potato, and carrot. Add to the blender but don't blend yet.

4. Rinse the pot, place it over high heat, and add the onion and garlic. Cook for 3 to 4 minutes, adding water 1 tablespoon at a time to prevent burning. Transfer to the blender. Puree everything until smooth. Scrape the sides and continue blending as needed. Pour the cheese sauce into the pot and place it over medium heat. Cook, stirring, until the sauce comes to a simmer.

5. Use immediately, or refrigerate in a sealable container for up to 1 week.

Per Serving (½ cup) Calories: 191; Fat: 10g; Protein: 9g; Carbohydrates: 20g; Fiber: 4g

MILD HARISSA SAUCE

Prep time: 10 minutes ★ **Cook time:** 20 minutes ★ **Makes:** 3 to 4 cups

NUT-FREE **QUICK**

Harissa is a North African and Middle Eastern hot chile paste. This recipe is an inspired version of harissa because it uses roasted red bell peppers in place of spicy peppers to create a sauce anyone can enjoy. Roasting the red pepper, onion, and garlic caramelizes their natural sugars to create a hint of sweet paired with a slight smokiness. If you like spice, add a variety of chile peppers, like jalapeño, serrano, or even habanero, to your roasting pan. This sauce is a delicious topping for salads, grain bowls, or hummus.

1 large red bell pepper, seeded, cored, and cut into chunks

1 yellow onion, cut into thick rings

4 garlic cloves, peeled

1 cup no-sodium vegetable broth or water

2 tablespoons tomato paste

1 tablespoon low-sodium soy sauce or tamari

1 tablespoon Hungarian paprika

1 teaspoon ground cumin

1. Preheat the oven to 450°F. Line a baking sheet with parchment paper or aluminum foil.

2. Place the bell pepper on the prepared baking sheet, flesh-side up, and space out the onion and garlic around the pepper.

3. Roast on the middle rack for 20 minutes. Transfer to a blender.

4. Add the vegetable broth, tomato paste, soy sauce, paprika, and cumin. Puree until smooth. Served cold or warm.

5. Refrigerate in an airtight container for up to 2 weeks or freeze for up to 6 months.

Tip: This recipe is intentionally mild to allow for customization based on your personal spice preference. Add any hot peppers you like to the roasting pan with the bell pepper, onion, and garlic. Roasting the hot peppers keeps the spice but enhances their natural flavor.

Per Serving (¼ cup) Calories: 15; Fat: <1g; Protein: 1g; Carbohydrates: 3g; Fiber: 1g

COCONUT "BACON" BITS

Prep time: 15 minutes ★ **Cook time:** 12 minutes, plus time to cool ★ **Makes:** 2 cups

GLUTEN-FREE

When people describe the taste of bacon, the two most prevalent flavors are "salty" and "smoky." This recipe doesn't try to mimic bacon, but it does capture those two flavors. These little bits of crunchy, seasoned, and toasted coconut are a simple way to elevate a salad, soup, or even pancake stack. One of the best uses is on a gooey peanut butter sandwich.

2 tablespoons tamari or low-sodium soy sauce

1 tablespoon liquid hickory smoke

1 tablespoon pure maple syrup

½ teaspoon smoked paprika

¼ teaspoon onion powder

¼ teaspoon ground white pepper

2 cups unsweetened coconut flakes (not desiccated)

1. Preheat the oven to 350°F. Line a baking sheet with parchment paper or aluminum foil. Avoid using a silicone mat, because the ingredients will stain the surface.

2. In a large bowl, stir together the tamari, liquid smoke, maple syrup, paprika, onion powder, and ground white pepper. Add the coconut flakes. Stir and toss gently to combine until the coconut flakes are thoroughly coated. Let sit for 10 minutes. Stir again, then spread the coconut evenly on the prepared baking sheet.

3. Bake for 12 minutes. The coconut flakes should look dry and golden brown rather than dark.

4. Let cool completely on the baking sheet.

5. Store in an airtight container at room temperature for 2 weeks or freeze for up to 2 months.

Tip: Using coconut flakes is the key to this recipe. Desiccated coconut will toast too quickly and the texture is too gritty and grainy once toasted.

Per Serving (1 tablespoon) Calories: 36; Fat: 3g; Protein: 1g; Carbohydrates: 2g; Fiber: 1g

CILANTRO & LIME CHUTNEY

Prep time: 10 minutes ★ **Makes:** 1 cup

GLUTEN-FREE NO COOK NUT-FREE QUICK

Vibrantly green, fresh, flavorful, and aromatic, this popular Indian dipping sauce pairs well with both spicy and complex-tasting dishes—or as a simple spread to perk up naan or flatbread. The blend of fresh cilantro, lime, green chiles, ginger, and spices only gets better the longer it's in the refrigerator. Use it to boost flavors in a hummus, as a creamy dip or salad dressing, or as a marinade or topping for roasted root vegetables.

2 green chiles, stemmed

1 tablespoon grated peeled fresh ginger

1 teaspoon lime zest

Juice of 1 large lime

2 tablespoons water, plus more as needed

2 cups fresh cilantro, washed and shaken dry

1 tablespoon agave syrup, or pure maple syrup

½ teaspoon ground cumin

¼ teaspoon ground coriander

1. In a blender, combine the green chiles, ginger, lime zest and juice, and 2 tablespoons of water. Puree until smooth.

2. Add the cilantro, agave syrup, cumin, and coriander. Puree again until smooth. Scrape down the sides, as needed, and add up to 2 tablespoons more water to reach your desired consistency.

3. Refrigerate in an airtight container for up to 2 weeks or freeze for up to 6 months.

Tip: Chaat masala is a common spice added to this chutney, but, unless you have access to an Indian grocery store, it is difficult to find. Chaat masala is similar to garam masala but it contains mango powder, which adds an acidic taste.

Per Serving (1 tablespoon) Calories: 8; Fat: 0g; Protein: <1g; Carbohydrates: 2g; Fiber: <1g

CORN BREAD MUFFINS

Prep time: 10 minutes ★ **Cook time:** 20 minutes ★ **Makes:** 12 muffins

NUT-FREE QUICK

Corn bread muffins seem like an unlikely staple, but if you're making a hearty chili or soup, corn bread is a necessity. Corn's natural sweetness makes these muffins a good addition to a savory breakfast hash, or even crumbled over a bowl of oatmeal. Most corn bread muffins rely on a lot of sugar and butter or oil for flavor and structure. The salt is optional, but the flavor will be slightly altered without it.

Oil, for preparing the muffin pan (optional)

½ cup canned corn

1½ cups unsweetened oat milk or other nondairy milk

¼ cup agave syrup or pure maple syrup

¼ cup unsweetened applesauce

1¼ cups whole wheat flour

1 cup cornmeal

4 teaspoons baking powder

½ teaspoon salt (optional)

1. Preheat the oven to 400°F. Lightly coat a muffin pan with oil, or line it with parchment paper.

2. In a large bowl, mash the corn slightly with a potato masher or heavy spoon. Stir in the oat milk, agave syrup, and applesauce.

3. In a medium bowl, whisk together the flour, cornmeal, baking powder, and salt (if using) to combine. Using a spatula, fold the dry ingredients into the wet ingredients until combined. Evenly divided the batter among the prepared muffin cups.

4. Bake for 16 to 20 minutes. The tops of the muffins should be lightly browned, and a toothpick inserted into the middle of a muffin should come out clean. Let cool for 5 minutes before transferring the muffins to a wire rack to cool completely.

5. Store in a resealable bag or airtight container at room temperature for up to 1 week or freeze for 1 to 2 months.

Tip: These muffins are a little drier than typical corn muffins. However, the standard bakery corn bread muffin contains 8 grams of refined sugar and 10 grams of saturated fat. This recipe uses agave syrup, which adds sweetness but isn't as glycemic spiking as refined sugar. If you want gluten-free muffins, replace the whole wheat flour one-to-one with a gluten-free baking mix.

Per Serving (1 muffin) Calories: 121; Fat: 2g; Protein: 3g; Carbohydrates: 25g; Fiber: 2g

WFPB GRANOLA

Prep time: 15 minutes ⋆ **Cook time:** 25 minutes ⋆ **Makes:** 8 cups

`GLUTEN-FREE` `QUICK`

This granola has fewer than half the calories per serving of most store-bought granolas and gives you morning energy without the sugar crash later. Chia seeds and dates sweeten the oats, keep them crisp, and make delectable little clumps. Combining chia seeds and ground flaxseed gives you omega fatty acids, soluble fiber, and protein. Typically, a serving of granola is a skimpy ½ cup, but using whole-food, plant-based ingredients means you can enjoy a full cup.

½ cup aquafaba (canned chickpea water)

½ teaspoon cream of tartar

½ cup pitted Medjool dates

1 tablespoon chia seeds

½ teaspoon vanilla extract

3 cups old-fashioned rolled oats or certified gluten-free oats

1 cup unsweetened coconut flakes

¼ cup pecans, coarsely chopped

¼ cup sliced almonds

1 tablespoon ground flaxseed

1 teaspoon ground cinnamon

½ cup dried cranberries or dried-fruit blend

¼ cup sunflower seeds

¼ cup pumpkin seeds

1. Preheat the oven to 350°F. Line a baking sheet with parchment paper.

2. In a food processor or high-speed blender, combine the aquafaba and cream of tartar. Process for 1 to 2 minutes until thick and foamy. Add the dates and chia seeds. Puree for about 1 minute until completely incorporated. Scrape down the sides and add the vanilla. Process for 30 seconds. Set aside.

3. In a large bowl, stir together the oats, coconut, pecans, almonds, flaxseed, and cinnamon, stirring well. Pour in the date mixture and stir until the oats are covered. Spread the granola onto the prepared baking sheet, but allow it to have some clumps.

4. Bake for 15 minutes. Using a spatula, turn over the granola and gently mix it without breaking up the clumps. Flipping it helps the granola crisp without burning. Bake for 10 minutes more. The granola might feel slightly damp, but it will crisp as it cools. Let the granola cool completely.

5. Stir in the cranberries, sunflower seeds, and pumpkin seeds.

6. Store in an airtight container at room temperature for up to 2 weeks or freeze for up to 2 months. Do not refrigerate, as it cause the oats to soften.

Tip: Aquafaba is the liquid from a can of chickpeas, and it has become popular as an egg substitute in many vegan baked-goods recipes. The proteins and fiber in the liquid are able to whip to a soft peak with a little cream of tartar, and this works as an oil substitute here for this granola—the chickpea proteins coat the oats and keep them crispy.

Per Serving (1 cup) Calories: 358; Fat: 18g; Protein: 8g; Carbohydrates: 46g; Fiber: 9g

SAVORY CHIA CRACKERS

Prep time: 20 minutes ★ **Cook time:** 20 minutes ★ **Makes:** 36 crackers

`GLUTEN-FREE` `NUT-FREE`

These oil-free, gluten-free crackers combine the goodness of brown rice and oats instead of traditional refined white flour. They make the perfect addition to a crudités platter, pair well with Creamy Roasted Red Pepper Hummus (page 154) and Chickpea Guacamole (page 153), and work well to scoop up or crumble into your favorite soup.

½ cup oat flour

½ cup brown rice flour

¼ cup water

2 teaspoons nutritional yeast

1 teaspoon chia seeds

¼ teaspoon freshly ground black pepper

¼ teaspoon onion powder

1. Preheat the oven to 350°F. Cut 2 sheets of parchment paper the size of your baking sheet. Place them on a work surface.

2. In a food processor, combine the oat and brown rice flours, water, nutritional yeast, chia seeds, pepper, and onion powder. Process for 1 to 2 minutes to combine into a dough. You should be able to pinch the dough between two fingers without it sticking to you.

3. Place the dough on one of the sheets of parchment paper. Using your clean hands, press the dough together into a mound, then press to flatten and shape into a thick square. Place the other sheet of parchment paper on top. Using a rolling pin, evenly flatten the dough to ⅛ inch thick. If your dough is too thick, the crackers won't be crispy. Remove the top sheet of parchment paper and save it for another use.

4. Using a knife or pizza cutter, cut the dough into 36 (1-by-2-inch) rectangles. Using a fork, lightly prick holes in the center of each cracker. Carefully transfer the parchment paper with the dough on it to a baking sheet.

5. Bake for 10 minutes. Carefully flip the crackers and bake for 10 minutes more until golden brown on the edges. Transfer the crackers to a wire rack to cool. They will crisp as they cool.

6. Store in an airtight container at room temperature for up to 1 week or freeze for up to 1 month.

Tip: You can purchase oat flour at most grocery stores. Do not assume that oat flour is gluten-free unless it says so on the label. If you are unable to find gluten-free oat flour, make your own by putting gluten-free oats into a food processor and blending for several minutes, or until the oats break down into a flour consistency.

Per Serving (4 crackers) Calories: 61; Fat: 1g; Protein: 2g; Carbohydrates: 12g; Fiber: 1g

CREAMY MUSHROOM GRAVY

Prep time: 10 minutes ⋆ **Cook time:** 15 minutes ⋆ **Makes:** 3 cups

`NUT-FREE` `ONE POT` `QUICK`

Gravy is seemingly a simple sauce, but it can make or break a family get-together. The rich flavors of this whole-food, plant-based gravy are built in steps, browning vegetables to bring out umami notes, then mixing with an easy cream sauce that is based on a standard béchamel sauce.

8 ounces baby portabella mushrooms, diced

4 ounces shiitake mushrooms, stemmed and diced

1 small yellow onion, diced

1 garlic clove, minced

1 tablespoon water, plus more as needed

3 tablespoons whole wheat flour

2 tablespoons tamari or coconut aminos

½ teaspoon freshly ground black pepper

¼ teaspoon ground white pepper

2 cups oat milk

1. In a large sauté pan or skillet over medium-high heat, cook the portabella and shiitake mushrooms for 3 to 5 minutes, or until all their moisture evaporates and the edges of the mushrooms begin to blacken. Add the onion and garlic. Cook for 5 minutes more, adding water, 1 tablespoon at a time, to prevent burning. The onion should be browned.

2. Stir in the flour, tamari, black pepper, and white pepper, stirring to coat and combine the cooked vegetables.

3. Pour in the milk. Cook, whisking, until the gravy bubbles. Turn the heat to low and cook for 5 minutes, whisking occasionally, until the gravy thickens.

4. Serve fresh or reheat as needed. Refrigerate in a sealable glass container for up to 1 week or freeze for up to 4 months. (Glass is preferred for freezing liquids because metal containers tend to leach a metallic taste.)

Tip: Have all the ingredients measured and ready before cooking, because there is little transition time.

Per Serving (½ cup) Calories: 81; Fat: 1g; Protein: 4g; Carbohydrates: 15g; Fiber: 3g

TOFU CREAM CHEESE

Prep time: 35 minutes ★ **Makes:** 2 cups

`5-INGREDIENT` `GLUTEN-FREE` `NO COOK` `NUT-FREE`

This creamy, rich, and cheesy spread is good for schmearing on bagels, as a dip for raw veggies, and as a substitute for cream cheese in many recipes. The true treat is all the creative add-ins you can experiment with, like chopped sun-dried tomatoes, dried dill, jalapeño pepper, garlic, or even fresh berries. The extra-firm tofu gives you a serving of a complete protein without the fat. The salt is optional, but the flavor will be slightly altered without it.

1 (14-ounce) package water-packed extra-firm tofu

1 tablespoon nutritional yeast

1 tablespoon apple cider vinegar

1 teaspoon yellow (mellow) miso paste

1 teaspoon pure maple syrup or agave syrup

½ teaspoon salt (optional)

1. Drain and press the tofu to remove excess moisture: Wrap the tofu in a clean kitchen towel or several paper towels and place a cutting board on top. Put 2 (28-ounce) cans on the cutting board directly above the tofu to add weight, which will expel the liquid. Let sit for at least 30 minutes.

2. In a high-speed blender or food processor, combine the pressed tofu, nutritional yeast, vinegar, miso paste, maple syrup, and salt, if using. Puree until smooth.

3. If you are adding flavorings (see headnote), stir them in and refrigerate for at least 1 hour or overnight to develop the flavors.

4. Serve immediately, or refrigerate in a sealable container for up to 2 weeks.

Tip: The extra-firm, water-packed tofu provides a thicker consistency, and it can be pressed to remove excess moisture. Silken tofu will fall apart if you press it.

Per Serving (2 tablespoons) Calories: 29; Fat: 1g; Protein: 3g; Carbohydrates: 1g; Fiber: <1g

REFRIGERATOR PICKLES

Prep time: 20 minutes, plus overnight to chill ★ **Cook time:** 10 minutes ★ **Makes:** 2 pints

GLUTEN-FREE NUT-FREE

This recipe isn't WFPB, but these pickles are far healthier—and tastier!—than most store-bought pickles. They also help bump up the flavor of other recipes for a fraction of the salt and sugar cost. Usually, making pickles at home requires special canning equipment and a waiting period of several months. Bypass all of that using your refrigerator and a highly acidic brine. You can even get creative—replace the cucumbers with zucchini or yellow summer squash. The result is cool, crisp pickles ready for your next backyard cookout.

1 pound small cucumbers, preferably pickling cucumbers, washed and dried

1 small yellow onion, chopped or cut into rings

1 cup apple cider vinegar

1 cup water

¼ cup beet sugar

1 tablespoon kosher salt

1 tablespoon pickling spice

1. Using a sharp knife or mandoline, cut the unpeeled cucumbers into ¼-inch-thick rounds.

2. In a large bowl, toss together the cucumbers and onion to evenly mix. Divide the mixture between 2 widemouthed 1-pint canning jars with lids, leaving ½ inch of headspace at the top where the lid rings begin, and pack them in using your clean hand or a heavy spoon. Be careful not to break the cucumbers.

3. In a small pot over high heat, combine the vinegar, water, beet sugar, salt, and pickling spice. Bring to a boil, stirring, and cook until the sugar and salt dissolve. Pour the brine over the vegetables, leaving ½ inch of headspace at the top. You might not use all the brine. Loosely screw on the lids and gently tap the jars on the counter a couple of times to remove any air bubbles. If necessary, add more brine to fill the jars to the ½-inch line, then secure the lids tightly. Let the jars cool to room temperature.

4. Refrigerate for at least 24 hours before serving. These pickles will have even more flavor over time and they will retain a crisper texture than their grocery store cousins.

5. Due to the high acid content in the brine, you can keep these pickles refrigerated for 1 month or longer; however, because they did not go through a canning process, they are not shelf-stable.

Tip: Get creative with flavorings: Add spicy peppers, bell peppers, garlic, or other spices to individual jars. The amount of sugar and salt may seem like a lot, but you aren't drinking the brine or eating an entire jar of pickles in one sitting.

Per Serving (4 pickles) Calories: 218; Fat: 1g; Protein: 4g; Carbohydrates: 50g; Fiber: 7g

MOCHA-WALNUT CASHEW BUTTER

Prep time: 10 minutes ✶ **Cook time:** 20 minutes, plus 15 minutes to cool ✶ **Makes:** 2 cups

GLUTEN-FREE

Homemade nut butter simply tastes better. It has a more complex flavor and an intoxicating aroma largely because the time between roasting and enjoying is minutes compared to the weeks or months of store-bought products. Making it at home allows you to get creative with flavors and nut blends and control the sugar and salt content. This version tastes great on toast or added to your favorite smoothie for protein and flavor.

2 cups raw cashews

1 cup raw walnuts

3 tablespoons cacao powder

2 tablespoons pure maple syrup

1 teaspoon vanilla extract

1 teaspoon instant coffee grounds or espresso powder

2 tablespoons nut-based oil (optional, see tip)

1. Preheat the oven to 350°F.

2. Spread the cashews and walnuts on a baking sheet and bake for 10 minutes. Shake the sheet, then bake for 5 to 10 minutes more until golden brown. Let cool for 15 minutes.

3. Transfer the toasted nuts to a food processor or high-speed blender. Add the cacao powder, maple syrup, vanilla, and instant coffee. Process until crumbly, scrape down the sides, and continue to process until smooth. The amount of time it takes for your nut butter to go from a thick ball to creamy smooth depends on your equipment. A high-speed blender might take only 2 minutes, whereas a food processor can take up to 10 minutes.

4. Transfer to a sealable container like a widemouthed mason jar.

Tip: If your nut butter isn't getting creamy as indicated in step 3, add the nut-based oil, or other neutral oil. Olive oil has too potent a flavor and coconut oil turns solid at room temperature. Never add water because it will make the nut butter turn rancid on the shelf and can cause the nut butter to seize while processing.

Per Serving (1 tablespoon) Calories: 72; Fat: 6g; Protein: 2g; Carbohydrates: 4g; Fiber: 1g

measurement conversions

VOLUME EQUIVALENTS	U.S. STANDARD	U.S. STANDARD [OUNCES]	METRIC [APPROXIMATE]
LIQUID	2 tablespoons	1 fl. oz.	30 mL
	¼ cup	2 fl. oz.	60 mL
	½ cup	4 fl. oz.	120 mL
	1 cup	8 fl. oz.	240 mL
	1½ cups	12 fl. oz.	355 mL
	2 cups or 1 pint	16 fl. oz.	475 mL
	4 cups or 1 quart	32 fl. oz.	1 L
	1 gallon	128 fl. oz.	4 L
DRY	⅛ teaspoon	–	0.5 mL
	¼ teaspoon	–	1 mL
	½ teaspoon	–	2 mL
	¾ teaspoon	–	4 mL
	1 teaspoon	–	5 mL
	1 tablespoon	–	15 mL
	¼ cup	–	59 mL
	⅓ cup	–	79 mL
	½ cup	–	118 mL
	⅔ cup	–	156 mL
	¾ cup	–	177 mL
	1 cup	–	235 mL
	2 cups or 1 pint	–	475 mL
	3 cups	–	700 mL
	4 cups or 1 quart	–	1 L
	½ gallon	–	2 L
	1 gallon	–	4 L

OVEN TEMPERATURES	FAHRENHEIT	CELSIUS [APPROXIMATE]
	250°F	120°C
	300°F	150°C
	325°F	165°C
	350°F	180°C
	375°F	190°C
	400°F	200°C
	425°F	220°C
	450°F	230°C

WEIGHT EQUIVALENTS	U.S. STANDARD	METRIC [APPROXIMATE]
	½ ounce	15 g
	1 ounce	30 g
	2 ounces	60 g
	4 ounces	115 g
	8 ounces	225 g
	12 ounces	340 g
	16 ounces or 1 pound	455 g

resources

The China Study: The Most Comprehensive Study of Nutrition Ever Conducted and the Startling Implications for Diet, Weight Loss, and Long-Term Health by **T. Colin Campbell and Thomas M. Campbell II**

The title really defines the book, a truly comprehensive study into nutrition and how radically we are affected by what we eat. This book started the whole-food, plant-based movement and is often used to explain the impact of this diet.

Eat Right. Academy of Nutrition and Dietetics (EatRight.org)

The Academy of Nutrition and Dietetics is the world's largest organization of food and nutrition professionals, and their website offers nutrition support and articles on the whole-food, plant-based diet.

Forks Over Knives (ForksOverKnives.com)

Hands down, this is my favorite online resource for recipe ideas. There's also a monthly magazine that is both beautiful and informative. If you're new to the whole-food, plant-based diet, check it out.

The How Not to Die Cookbook: 100+ Recipes to Help Prevent and Reverse Disease by **Michael Greger and Gene Stone**

This research-based book provides recipe and nutrition ideas for fighting specific diseases. A great resource to have in your cookbook collection.

In Defense of Food by **Michael Pollan**

This book offers insight into how we, as a society, have transitioned from food made in the kitchen to food products made by factories. Pollan has other books that focus more on nutrition and the history of food, but this is a good read if you're looking to understand our eating habits.

index

about the author

JUSTIN WEBER is from northern Wisconsin, has two children who are his most eager taste testers, and posts recipes and health tips on social media using the handle @CrowMoonKitchen.

NOTES

NOTES

NOTES

NOTES

NOTES

NOTES

NOTES

NOTES

NOTES

NOTES

NOTES

NOTES

NOTES